illusive

CONTEMPORARY
ILLUSTRATION
PART FOUR

gestalten

INTRODUCTION

BY JOHN O'REILLY

—

The rapid pace of change in the creative, commercial, and social spheres has generated uncertainty among illustrators, art directors, and brands. But with imagination and creativity, illustrators are mapping new ways of visualizing and experiencing our fast-changing world.

It is hard to imagine more uncertain or more exciting times for the art of illustration—risk and excitement often go hand-in-hand—and I wish I had an illustrator to picture the idea, the story, and emotional textures of this moment. Well in fact, here we have a book full of extraordinary image-makers doing just that.

Over the last decade, the creative industries have seen enormous disruption and perhaps none more so than the world of illustration, which has seen the familiar, linear commissioning hierarchies and fees of the print industries slowly recede and decline. Yet while one strand of illustration is disappearing, so many others are expanding at an incredible rate, giving illustration so many more purposes beyond that of looking good on the printed page. So while the printed page of newspapers and magazines is disappearing fast, illustration is mapping new territories and new forms for itself: on smartphone games and apps; on floors and walls of buildings; in diagramming scientific research; in the cartographies of urban planners and architecture; in mapping and directing thought processes in meetings and conferences; in making things and objects; and in disrupting the image and traditional animation itself in the GIF, as is the case with Christoph Niemann's classic covers for *The New Yorker,* which now play out in different formats online [p. 100]. This makes the creative task more challenging. How do you make an image that works as a static illustration and a moving GIF? This work highlights the new kind of adaptive creativity and image-making required in our multi-format age. Niemann is an archetype of this new kind of image-maker and it is no surprise that his style has been much imitated. But what makes his work so definitive and so effective is its lightness and mobility, its ability to traverse different spaces and make us think about digital and physical space.

It is not just the old outlets for illustrations that have this mix of uncertainty and extraordinary opportunity; it's the very notion of illustration itself. When *Varoom,* the magazine that I edit, was originally set up, the well-known, highly respected founders from the world of illustration and design considered giving it the strapline *Journal of the Made Image.* Not "Illustration" but the "Made Image," referring to the fact that illustration now encompasses so many different practices. It can be abstract and figurative, static and mobile, a picture and an object. You will see many examples of these different kinds of image-making throughout the book.

This uncertainty about naming a genre of imagery is far from a problem. Rather, it is a sign of exciting creative times; it's a sign of creativity and image-making working at the boundaries of collage, drawing, painting, lettering, mixed-media, and street art, as seen in Raymond Lemstra's little totems that visually mix the mechanic and the tribal, graphic figures whose construction tells a narrative [p. 156]. Contemporary illustrators are themselves often a mix of many different parts, creating different kinds of work for different platforms. They are, to use a term from Baudelaire, flâneurs.

This book highlights the complexity and diversity of contemporary illustration—which also makes telling this story a challenge— echoing the difficulties that illustrators, art buyers, and brands are slowly having to address. In an age when communication is being continually disrupted as our attention drops in and out of the screen devices we carry around at all times, how do illustrators and brands unfold a story (whether a traditional story, marketing story, product story, or brand story)? Like Adam Hayes's image of our ubiquitous communication devices, the proximity of everything can mean the proximity of nothing. In the media complexity of contemporary life, we create our own route through the oxygen of information that surrounds us. And this experience of complexity is expressed in some key visual themes and aesthetics.

The resurgence of interest in collage is partly because it effectively expresses the idea of knitting your own network together, creating an alternative path through reality by joining together different scraps of time. Collage is a popular form across editorial commissions (the business pages are a favored location), book publishers, and even fashion brands (especially stop-frame animation), as the essential chaos of collage captures the fluidity of our multi-channel experience of daily life. The illustrator holds this all together by an aesthetic combining the futuristic and the nostalgic: Martin O'Neill's faded washes of time [p 344]; Peter Horvath's jittery optimism of iconography, bodies, and technology [p. 314]; and Laurindo Feliciano's collaged covers for *Flaunt* magazine that feature characters who seem to be composing the very image we are looking at [p. 326, 329].

In art history, collage was initially seen as experimenting with issues of representation (in Braque and Picasso for example), or generating uncanny narratives (surrealism) from the perspective of a media philosopher such as Marshall McLuhan, the daily newspaper was a collage form made of photos, headlines, texts, typographies, and adverts, stories of politics and war or sport and celebrity cut and pasted alongside each other. McLuhan worked with designer Quentin Fiore to create works such as *The Medium is the Massage*, where the book is designed as a collage, and where collage is not just an aesthetic but a way of thinking. Collage demands participation; it encourages us to fill in the gaps. In an age where everything is visible, collage is the art of making the visible invisible. It gives us the pleasure of having to make new narrative and logical connections.

And indeed there is a new generation for whom sites such as Twitter and Tumblr are very immediate practices of collage—though digital commerce finds profit in sedimenting data—so Facebook's timeline seeks to order in linear fashion all the content we have collaged together. But, our media interactions on smartphones and laptops primarily make experience far less linear—jumping into archives, conversations, links, videos, or posting pictures. If for the surrealists collage was a way of accessing the dreamworld of the unconscious (cutting out shapes from found images also meant cutting

1.

out the given logic and context of a found image), then everyday life begins to take on the dynamic of our dreamworld with its random connections and leaps. Contemporary life generates a strange kind of storytelling whose aesthetic can be crunchy, such as in the geometric forms of Julien Pacaud's visual landscapes [p. 308], which slide different bits of time together; or in the sculptural digital collages of Mat Maitland, whose shiny images foreground the smooth uncanny dreamworld of brands, celebrity, and lifestyle objects [p. 320].

Whereas art critics have long criticized the appropriation of collage as a style, arguing that popular collage, unlike the surrealists', doesn't deliver a critical whole, contemporary collage is like a hyperlink, a switching point to take us somewhere else.

It is no surprise that the figure of the flâneur has begun to emerge as an inspiration in the design community. The idea of the flâneur is an idea that originated in Baudelaire's early vision of "The Painter of Modern Life," where he built his notion of the flâneur around the illustrator Constantin Guys. Guys was a figure intoxicated on the flow of life, in his passion for observing and absorbing change, someone interested in everything and everyone, even those considered to be trivial. In fact, Baudelaire writes, "I am prepared to go even further and assert that inspiration has something in common with a convulsion, and that every sublime thought is accompanied by a more or less violent shock which has its repercussion

1. PETER HORVATH – MOON UNDER MARTHA

1.

in the very core of the brain." This notion of the flâneur, politicized by philosopher Walter Benjamin, has become a key model for how we are as active citizens and consumers in the twenty-first century. Benjamin's depiction of the early twentieth-century flâneurs, the wanderers of the city who pick up information, fragments from here. And there in the city, this information takes them in new directions, and becomes a model of our mobile age with multiple screens, as we constantly jump from the physical to the virtual.

A commercial incarnation of the flâneur is the agency trend-spotter, who collages different cultural expressions in a narrative to develop a strategy for a client. But most of all, contemporary collage reflects and creates the very modern, fluid, flexible identity of the flâneur (it also plays into social/cultural issues of gender and the "Flexi-Sexual"). It is no surprise that recently we've seen the launch of the Berlin-originated *Flaneur* magazine, whose layouts that play with photography and typography, drawing and mapping, text and image, have garnered a cult following and critical success among the creative community. Fashion brand Hermès recently designated their theme of the year as the flâneur, with an accompanying exhibition of objects (called "Wanderland") from their archives. Indeed, collage has become a creative alternative to elaborate theatrical fashion photography. Liselotte Watkins's paper cutting and mixed media images explore color and construction, re-mythologizing the celebrity-led fashion image whose story is owned by the celebrity [p. 30]. Quentin Jones's surreal mix of black inky spills and collage turns the fashion image into a dark, unhinged cartoon of the psyche [p. 334]. The fragmented aesthetic of collage and its counterpoint in the flâneur is a way of addressing twenty-first century storytelling in an age where our experience of life has rapidly become non-linear. The flâneur is about discovery through the art of getting lost.

It is partly why we have seen a return to Letterpress and Letterpress-styles, an upsurge in interest in printing, and a contemporary folk aesthetic that taps into illustration's tradition of illustrated folk tales, while also delivering new arrangements that unsettle expectations of familiar stories: Anna and Elena Balbusso's pictures blur the line between the human and the natural world [p. 210]; Bjørn Rune Lie's image-making circulates a folk-style between his children's books and his editorial and advertising commissions [p. 368]. We can also see David Doran's love of print textures [p. 242]; Emma Löfström's hybrid forms [p. 74, 237]; Eero Lampinen's deceptively strange relations between humans and insect and plant life [p. 172]; and BMD Design's exquisitely drawn occult sigils and signs [p. 160]. There are other commercial factors driving this aesthetic. As traditional markets for illustration break down, illustrators are seeking to build portfolio incomes, one of which is selling prints both online and via quick gallery shows. Then there is also the growth of small independent publishers such as Nobrow, who publish graphic novels with an emphasis on a print aesthetic. Illustrators featured in this volume such as Bjørn Rune Lie and Raymond Lemstra cross-fertilize their graphic novel sensibility and work for commercial clients.

What's fascinating about all this work is the way it borrows and uses the visual language of folk culture, with its woods and creatures, while introducing subtle twists of scale or character. This work expresses creative ecological uncertainties and uses this uncertainty to create odd new visual mythologies—these worlds are not so distant from the energies and landscapes of David Lynch's *Twin Peaks,* soon to see a third season almost 25 years after the first two. It's not difficult to see why the cult TV series has been recommissioned, as it depicts a world where the distinct spaces between the rational and the irrational, the waking and the dream, and the natural and supernatural forces of order and disorder fold into each other. Just as the mythic quality of Twin Peaks emerges from the differences and connections between these worlds, a slice of contemporary illustration's mythic qualities echoes the gap we live in between the physical and the virtual, celebrating the diversity of identities and interests, curiosities and eccentricities that flow between web world and everyday life.

This uncertainty around the blended realities we currently move through is a rich source for illustrators, and is a driver of so much interesting work exploring space. Mireille Fauchon's collages for Spacewarp (during a residency for the London Design Festival, partnering with Slashstroke magazine and architectural interior designer Harriet Anstruther Studio) deconstruct the residency space and remake it as an abstract narrative that plays with our sense of inside and outside, entry points and exit points both in the architectural space and the image itself [p. 332]. Joe Iurato's wood cutouts insert unexpected stories in urban spaces, making us question what is an image, and where the boundary lies between image and reality [p. 102]. Images move freely between the imaginary and reality. Case in point is Christoph Niemann's slideshow of Kraftwerk for *Die Zeit*, which uses the photograph as a canvas, visualizing Kraftwerk's music as an image virus rewiring our minds and perception to see the space of everyday life differently [p. 98].

This flow between the fictional and the real is also driving experimental new forms in architectural image-making. Indeed, some of the most creative image-making is emerging from young architects seeking escape from the hyperrealism of high-powered computer-generated design. For instance, the extraordinary speculative fiction *Frackpool* by Jason Lamb imagines U.K. town Blackpool regenerated by repurposing its imaginary fracking industry (fuelled by Chinese investment) to become a sustainable city [p. 96]. The scale of the work, its pencil-drawn images, and the fluidity of its eastern and western aesthetic captures the power of illustration to engage with the impossible and make it real, to

give impossible worlds visual form. This is illustrated in Monument Valley, a smartphone game created by Ustwo. The game's designers explained that they wanted to create a game in which architecture wasn't just the background but was the main character. Who would have thought a game involving absurd architectures and impossible spaces, and inspired by M.C. Escher, would have proved so popular? By the end of January 2015, Ustwo had sold nearly 2.5 million Monument Valley games. It is fascinating that a game built around illustrating and disrupting space mirrors the fluid existential and professional spot currently occupied by illustration. Illustrators who are having to find, actually make, new commercial spaces for their work as the traditional markets disappear. The same can be said for art directors, art buyers, and brands in a post-advertising age, who have the opportunity to reimagine how they might use illustration to conceptualize (not just visualize) their brands, and how they might use the affective power of illustration to engage and disrupt the perception of their desired audience.

Another way of looking at it is this: think of illustration as a force or power with the capacity to change, and think of creative directors, designers, and brands as young Luke Skywalkers or (Anakins!) who haven't quite recognized the sheer scale of what illustration can do. The work in this book highlights illustrators using commercial and aesthetic uncertainty to develop novel styles and formats that map new directions for the illustrated image.

1. QUENTIN JONES – MINNIE THE MASKED   2. MIREILLE FAUCHON – SPACEWARP 3. JOE IURATO – SMALL WORLD

CONTEMPORARY ILLUSTRATION

—

1. NAJA CONRAD-HANSEN: VALENTINO

FASHION

As the photographic fashion image became ubiquitous alongside concerns about representation and Photoshopping, illustration has come to embody the experimental spirit of fashion.

The last decade has seen a huge revival in fashion illustration, from major museum shows at London's Design Museum and the Museum für Kunst und Gewerbe Hamburg to the use of illustration in mainstream fashion magazines; and from the special features on avant-garde fashion websites such as Nick Knight's Showstudio to the commissioning of illustrators by designers, magazines, and blogs to cover fashion weeks around the globe.

Vogue made its first non-illustration photographic cover in 1932, and over time illustration slowly disappeared from the pages of glossy fashion magazines. But at a moment when the very idea of the "fashion image" is being questioned, interest in it has exploded. It is partly a branding matter—in the age of social sharing, the fashion photograph feels less exclusive. It is partly an aesthetic and ethical issue: when consumers demonstrate concern over Photoshopped faces and bodies, illustrated images feel less existentially oppressive—they are clearly fictional. The bodies recede into the background; with fashion illustration it's about the clothes, or a concept of the clothes—their weight and movement, the dynamic of the drawing's line and color. A great fashion image is never static; it's always an image of transformation.

The use of contemporary illustration in the fashion industry plays into wider cultural questions around notions of the body. High-end fashion shoots have often challenged conventions of beauty—think Alexander McQueen and Nick Knight's controversial

shoot in the 1990s for *Dazed and Confused* magazine, featuring people with disabilities. Because fashion glories in its temporariness, in how we might transform ourselves, it has always had a more complex relationship to the body and its representation; the ethereality of the watercolor fashion image gestures toward exploring the ethereality of the fashion image in an age where there has never been more of them. The illustrators in the following pages each transform the idea of what the fashion image might be.

POST-REALISM

Drawings offer a different rhythm of engaging with the world, inspiring us to consider the relationship between picture and reality in the age of the image.

The surge in popular interest in drawing—in illustrators' performance of drawing at live events, in retailers and brands hiring illustrators such as Good Wives and Warriors to draw murals in their buildings—points to a minor obsession with drawing. It is partly because drawing itself is an obsessional activity, a process critic John Berger says we lose ourselves in. Or more strangely, the outside world loses itself in us as we map, trace, and give it form with pen and pencil. Drawing enables a wonderful circulation and play between our sense of what is inside and what is outside, and allows us to play with our fixed sense of image and reality.

3.

2. NAJA CONRAD-HANSEN: LANVIN WINTER 2015 ACCESSORIES COLLECTION 3. TIM LAING: VEVE

Like the surge in interest in analogue practices, it is easy to simply dismiss our current passion for drawing as some non-specific reaction to digital culture. But let's be less generic and consider a similar trend: the increasing popularity of vinyl culture.

With our MP3 player we simply click to play, touch and play. With vinyl we take the sleeve in our hands, slide out the inner sleeve, carefully balance the edge of the record in one hand between thumb and fingertips, align the hole in the vinyl with the nub on the record player, gently lower the needle, and find the groove. Like drawing, playing and listening to vinyl is the product of a whole set of physiological and technological relationships—to use an art term you might call it an assemblage—that slow things down, creating different rhythms within our fast-paced environment.

In the same way, much of the drawing in this section is about creating a decelerated, post-realist image that stretches time out, a different visual rhythm with more culturally dominant kinds of imagery.

This act of slowing things down is increasingly seen in illustrators' drawings on photographs, using the photograph itself as a canvas, like in Mario Hugo's work; his portrait of Rihanna uses the celebrity image as a canvas for publicity-as-graffiti [p. 107]. Or in the speculative realities of Emin Mete Erdoğan [p. 92] and Jason Lamb [p. 96]; or Florian Bayer's reportage pieces, where deeper layers of reality intrude [p. 110]; or Hvass and Hannibal's landscapes that are crystalline and futuristic [p. 60]. Post-realism is how illustrators document life, folding in the layers of images we carry around with us as humans in the age of pictures.

INFORMATION & GRAPHICS

As our lives become evermore saturated with information, illustrators are making images that connect and map the detail of the world.

Though information graphics boomed during the first decade of the new century, this form of visual ordering had a counterpart in what great editorial illustration always did—condensing the world through visual shorthand, crunching down a complex story into a single image. The editorial image orders the arguments and position around a story and will also give us an attitude. It's what distinguishes such imagery from information graphics. Harry Campbell's depiction of the mechanization of the sport of golf [p. 145], or Robert Samuel Hanson's image for the *New York Times*, the American bald eagle weighed down by fossil fuels [p. 127].

And whereas classic information graphics tend to picture large-scale socio-economic issues and stories, illustrators are mapping personal obsessions. For instance, Julene Harrison's "There is a Light" [p. 130] takes the information of the lyrics from the song by The Smiths and delivers it as a beautiful, painstakingly ornate paper cut piece.

1. ROBERT SAMUEL HANSON: KOREAN TACOS 2. CRISTINA AMODEO: SUMMER OBJECTS

The blade and cuttings at the bottom of the image testify to obsession. Mister Mourao's meticulous hand-drawn images of New York [p. 136], where the city itself disappears into the spectacularly detailed visual information of layer upon layer of lines, do so as well. As do David Sparshott's graphite and colored pencil deconstruction of a bicycle into its constituent elements [p. 134]. In these kinds of works, the illustrator breaks down the personal world into informational order.

Mapping by illustrators is also increasingly three-dimensional as clients tune into the sense of wonder that the creative artifice of small-scale models. See paper craft extraordinaire Hattie Newman's aesthetic for example, which is part perfectionist-prop-making and part old-school model-making [p. 118]. And in an age where information is the oxygen we swim in, mapping doesn't have to reduce complexity.

POP & REBELLION

Our time is defined by dissolving older certainties, and a new generation of illustrators and clients are creatively responding to cultural, economic, and technological disruption. Image-makers are discovering the fluid forms in 1960s and 1970s Pop Art, Op Art, and cartoons to re-shape how we make sense of change.

A younger generation of image-makers are looking to the imagery produced by an older generation who responded to the wave of change in the 1960s and 1970s, to Pop Art, Op Art, and Psychedelia, to recalibrate our eyes in order to grasp this fast-changing world. Marshall McLuhan, the great pop philosopher of the 1960s— a dazzling eccentric oracle to academics, artists, and business people of the time—wrote that, "when you step up the environment to those speeds, you create the psychedelic thrill. The whole world becomes kaleidoscopic."

You can see the traces of Jodorowsky and Moebius (Jean Giraud) in the cartoon-inflected work of many of the illustrators in this book. For Jodorowsky and Moebius, westerns and sci-fi flicks, fantasy creatures and robots, the mythic and the scientific, are the figures and shapes of hallucinatory, transformative imagery. In a 2010 interview with *Les Inrockuptibles* magazine, Moebius revealingly reflected upon change, and the alternate realities he and his imagery built and inhabited: "It was vital for me to take a pseudonym; I needed a password to navigate from one world to the other and to be able to come back... What interests me is rather the difficulty to keep one's identity and shape through metamorphosis. It might come from my bipolar nature but I always had trouble keeping stable forms."

Most notable is the sheer uninhibited use of color and shape, at the edge of visual madness, a hallucinatory enthusiasm for imagery that compacts and condenses accelerated social, cultural and technological change into fluid forms. The current wave of the psychedelic-pop color explosion is driven by millenials who have grown up in the smooth digitized world of the internet at the heart of liquid times_let's call this generation the Liquid Generation. It's a generation of image-makers inspired by the ubiquity of Street Art, and the typographic and aesthetic metamorphoses of these forms. It's a psychic rebellion against fixed visual forms.

The playful folly, the figurative madness and visual are the perceptual tools created by young illustrators giving us new shapes and perspectives with which to see the world. This is an imagery that liquefies, dissolves, and moves, with a visual energy and playful optimism that stays one step ahead of the uncertainty of change.

3.

3. TONI HALONEN: KENZOPEDIA – KENZO ROYAL BLUE

designers taking an interest in nostalgia: their study "Creatively Designing with/for Cultural Nostalgia" cites research showing how nostalgia can be regarded as a mechanism that enables social adaptation. You can see how in times of rapid change nostalgia and nostalgic imagery serve a social function.

But for illustrators, the return to an earlier form of image-making is also a way of playing with ideas of cool, and though we think cool is the expression of the emotionally languid and careless, cool is always exaggerated and mannered. When illustrators get to play with cool like in Tom Haugomat's image that nods to the idea of Big Brother [p. 271], they pay homage, smile, and topicalize the cliché and formula of cool.

And then there's Thomas Danthony's images of Los Angeles [p. 310], which are classic in the sense that they mesh geography and culture, as if the fictional city of Film Noir, with its heightened and reversible moral boundaries of good and evil, could only be visualized by the aesthetic of negative space. We may be hooked on classics but contemporary illustrators are rethinking the idea of the classic for their own practice.

COLLAGE

In an age where our lives are fragmented across digital and physical spaces, contemporary collage visualizes the beauty and pleasure of dislocation.

For the image-maker, the art of collage has always been the extended creative art of navigating the time of an elongated creative process, punctuated by an act of violence in the destruction of images. The collage artist inhabits many different identities along the way. There's the collector, the archivist, the cutter, the curator of fragments, and the fixer pasting it all together. For analogue collagists, the act of collage is often a psychological journey involving trips to flea markets or, nowadays to eBay lots, flicking through old magazines, or boxes of photographs and postcards. The act of collage can involve transforming private memories into art materials or cutting into someone else's past—the collage as an entry point to a world belonging to an other.

The collage images in the following pages all generate a sense of otherness, of anatomies (Bedelegeuse, p. 304), landscapes (Mireille Fauchon, p. 332) and distorted history (Peter Horvath, p. 314). Indeed, collage is also the art of dislocation, taking slices of time and relocating them.

CLASSICS

Contemporary illustrators are increasingly drawn to playing with the classics, connecting with nostalgia and cool.

Why are we hooked on classics? Why do we love contemporary illustration that looks like it's from the 1930s, 1940s, or 1950s? When you look at images by Telegramme, the ad for Percival clothes [p. 266] feels like a cool, contemporary version of Tintin. Or look at Mads Berg's image for an Italian liqueur [p. 275] that harks back to Herbert Matter's classic travel posters of the 1920s, the Art Deco geometry of the industrial age replaced by the glitch of the digital age. Some of what is driving this is indeed postmodern nostalgia. Swiss physician Johannes Hofer coined the term "nostalgia" in 1688 to describe the psychological effect on Swiss mercenaries of extended periods away from home—nostalgia as a kind of homesickness, a desire for an idealized past. The word nostalgia collages two greek words: *nostos* (homecoming), and *algos* (pain). Haian Xue from the Aalto University School of Arts, Design and Architecture, and Martin Woolley from Coventry School of Art and Design are among many

1. ELENI KALOPKOTI: GLITCH 2. HIFUMIYO: DAS MAGAZIN

Within art history, collage walks hand-in-hand with surrealism. This feeling that collage uniquely generates is also strangely futuristic: the history of collage in the early twentieth century was partly the result of new production technologies enabling the distribution and consumption of mass consumer goods. The second surge of collage came during the slow growth of consumerism in the West after the Second World War. In a series of recordings in the 1960s and 1970s, author, artist, man-with-scissors William Burroughs reflected upon his cut-up techniques saying that, "when you cut into the present, the future leaks out."

This future isn't something that follows the present. It is the alternative possibilities and impossibilities that exist within the present that the collage artist makes visible, and that's why collage is currently so popular. In our increasingly information-filled, non-linear everyday lives, where we jump-cut from our digital lives in the screens of smartphones to real life, collage signals the strange beauty in complexity. Contemporary collage is the art of dislocation, mapping the dislocated urgency of contemporary life.

STORYTELLING

In the age of multiple platforms and fragmented communications, the illustrator's talent for storytelling is much prized.

Depending on which story guru you ask (Hollywood scriptwriter, Jungian therapist, brand consultant...) every story is structured by timeless elements such as the hero, the journey, the testing of character, the revelation ("Luke, I am your Father!") and some sort of return. Except that in the digital age there are so many new product channels and contact points all requiring different formats and targeting different audiences, that the nature of storytelling is changing and becoming more fragmented.

The idea of the linear beginning and ending is having to fight for its place in the age of digression and hyperlinks. Stories in the twenty-first century begin in the middle—they begin wherever you are—and luckily for illustrators their kind of image construction and composition lends itself to this. Hifu Miyo's images borrow the language of the cinema close-up [p. 358] to expand the story in many directions through simple detail: the handwritten letter, the fountain pen, and the spectacles all clue us into a certain kind of character. Or the slightly Hitchcockian moment of the man looking down at his watch, an innocuous act except that the simple positioning of perspective suggests some kind of anxiety.

While children's books have a long tradition of playing with expectations, in recent years they have become even more experimental. Jon Klassen's *This is Not My Hat* won the Kate Greenaway medal in 2014, upending the conventions of what we might expect from children's books, delivering a surprisingly dark resolution defying the required happy ending [p. 354]. But because the characters (big fish, little fish, crab) are drawn with a degree of impishness around the dynamics of scale, we're primed (spoiler alert!) to be accepting of the fish's fate. Likewise, Chris Haughton's award-winning work "Shh We Have A Plan!" [p. 385] plays with the formula of the journey, but happily engages with chaos and failure.

In the age of multiple platforms, the illustrator's skill to deliver storytelling drama in single-panels and to place us immediately in the middle of a story is proving an immensely timely skill.

2.

2.

3.

4.   5.

1., 2. & 5. CASHIQUE S/S 15 3. WINTER MOT 4. BREAKFAST AT TIFFANY'S

1.

2.

3.

4.

LOVISA
BURFITT
—

1.

2.

3.

4.

1. VALISE 2. BALMAIN SS 2015 3. NICE 2013 4. MADAME BLUEHAIR 5. VALENTINO MAY 6. GIVENCHY SS 2015

LOVISA BURFITT

5.

6.

NAJA
CONRAD-HANSEN
—

1. DIOR HAIR 2. ANN DEMEULEMEESTER FW 2015

2.

NH 2015

SARAH
HOWELL
—

1. BACALL 2. THE BEARDED LADY

FASHION

2.

1.

ROSIE
MCGUINNESS
—

1. SHADES 2. TANK DRESS

2.

Prada   Valentino   Hermès

1.

2.

3.

1. LINE-UP 2. SUN HAT 3. JUMPSUIT 4. VALENTINO

Valentino

2.

3.

4.

5.

1. GETTING HITCHED WITHOUT A HITCH 2. GEMINI 3. SHE COVER 4. TIFFANY 5. GARDEN

1. PEONY 2. PED 3. NOCTURNE 4. MIGRATION

SHAINA ANDERSON | FASHION

LISELOTTE
WATKINS
—

1. & 2. L'OFFICIEL ITALIA

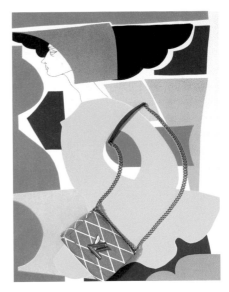

2.

1.

2.

3.

1. – 4. PODEO MAGAZINE

MARIA
RAYMONDSDOTTER
—

1.

1. THE CURIOUS HIPSTER 2. LABEL JUNKIE

FASHION

2.

1.

1. & 5. AGL SHOES – SS15 2. AGL SHOES – FW14 3. & 4. ILLUSTRATIONS II

2.

3.

4.

5.

ΛGL

1.

HELEN
BULLOCK
—

1. BOTTEGA VENETA 2. MISSONI

1.

3.

2.

4.

CECILIA
CARLSTEDT
—

1. & 2. PERSONAL 3. H&M 4. REFINERY 29

1. – 4. LONDON FASHION WEEK

4.

TINA
BERNING
—

1. QUEEN 1 2. TREATMENT 3. ELENA FERRANTE / THE GUARDIAN 4. STELLA

LE ROI M'A CHARGÉE

1. THOSE WHO STAY I 2. QUEEN 3. COLLIN 4. QUEEN IV

4.

2.

PAULA
SANZ CABALLERO
—
1. CORSET FOR RIJKSMUSEUM 2. MARGHERITA MISSONI FOR LUFTHANSA

1.

LESLEY
BARNES
—

1.

2.

1. FASHIONARY 2. V&A CHRISTMAS CARD 3. V&A: THE GLAMOUR OF ITALIAN FASHION

FASHION

1. & 2. V&A: THE GLAMOUR OF ITALIAN FASHION 3. CLINIQUE SUPERPRIMERS

3.

L.

ORIANA
FENWICK
—

1. CHRISTIAN NOBOA 2. WALTER AYOVI

POST REALISM

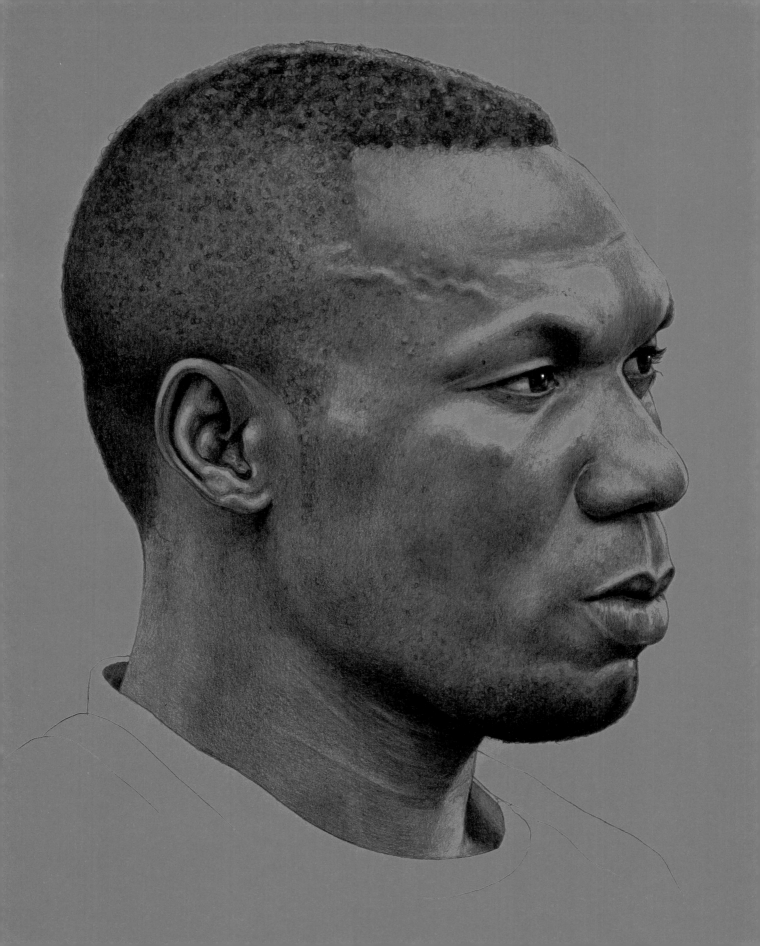

1.

2.

3.

1. PHILIPPE MALOUIN 2. WHY SCHIZOPHRENIA DOESN'T EXIST 3. THERAPIE UND MEDIKAMENTE/THERAPY AND MEDICATION
4. CHARLOTTE GAINSBOURG PORTRAIT

ORIANA FENWICK | POST REALISM

4.

1.

2.

3.

HVASS
& HANNIBAL
—

1. – 4. MONKI

POST REALISM

1.

POST REALISM

2.

ANDREAS
LIE
—

WOODLAND ANIMALS: 1. OBSERVING BEAR 2. WOODLAND WOLF 2

2.

3.

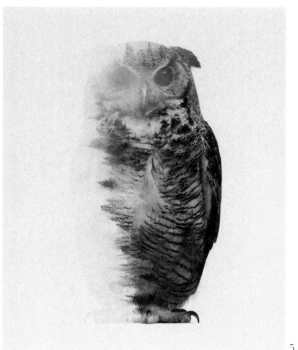

4. 5.

WOODLAND ANIMALS: 1. WOODLAND WOLF 2. WOODLAND FOX 3. WOODLAND LYNX 4. BISON 5. WOODLAND OWLLS

POST REALISM

1.

2.

SUTHIPA
KAMYAM
—

1. THE WEATHEP DIAPIES, PAVEN ILLUSTPATION OF NOPDIC FASHION BIENNALE 2014 FPANKFUPT, GEPMANY
2. UNTITLED, ILLUSTPATION FOP BOOK, ONCE UBON A TIME BY BENZ THANACHAPT

1. OLD WEATHERED VINES 2. "THE OLD SKIN" FROM A STORY OF CASSOWARY IN THE DEEP FOREST

SUTHIPA KAMYAM | POST REALISM

2.

CRISTINA
AMODEO
—

1. SUMMEP OBJECTS 2. CAMELLIA IMBPICATA MACPOPHYLLA

POST PEALISM

1.

HERBARIUM CAMELLIA: 1. SASANQUA 2. PICCIOLI 3. JAPONICA COMUNE 4. SUMMER OBJECTS – CORAL 5. JAPONICA SUPERIORE

CRISTINA AMODEO | POST REALISM

2.

3.

4.

5.

EMMA
LÖFSTRÖM
—

1. VANILLA 2. TEA

POST REALISM

1.

CARTER
ASMANN
—

COFFEE RING DRAWINGS: 1. HARLEY-DAVIDSON HYDRA-GLIDE 2. BMW CX500 3. BMW R100 4. BMW R32 5. HARLEY DAVIDSON XL100 6. DUCATI 900SS 7. HONDA CB550

2.

3.

4.

5.

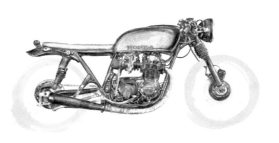

6.

7.

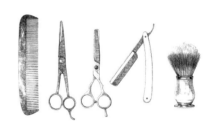

1. VILLANDRY 2. DUCK ISLAND COTTAGE & LOCK 3. THE RITZ 4. ARCHIVE COLLECTION

POST REALISM

LUCILLE
CLERC
—

5.

6.

5. & 6. SCHLOSS HOHENKAMMER

THOMAS
DANTHONY
—

1.

ALICE
TYE
—

THE LOST SHOPS OF SOHO: 1. FRATELLI CAMISA, OLD COMPTON STREET 2. RANDALL AND AUBIN BUTCHERS, 16 BREWER STREET

POST REALISM

THE LOST SHOPS OF SOHO: 1. HAMBURGER PRODUCTS, 1 BREWER STREET 4. RICHARD'S FISH SHOP, 11 BREWER STREET 5. PARMIGIANI FIGLIO, 36 OLD COMPTON STREET. 2. & 3. PEGGY GUGGENHEIM

43 G. PARMIGIANI FIGLIO

5.

1.

LEAH
FUSCO
—

1. M25 2. NATIONAL GRID SUBSTATION

POST REALISM

2.

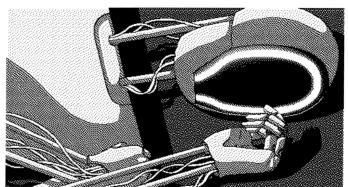

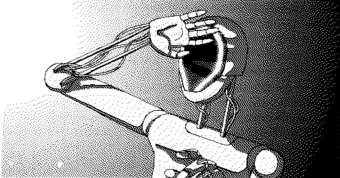

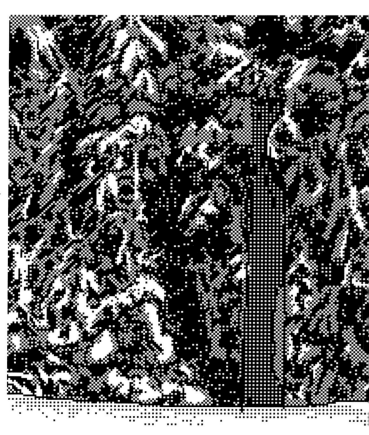

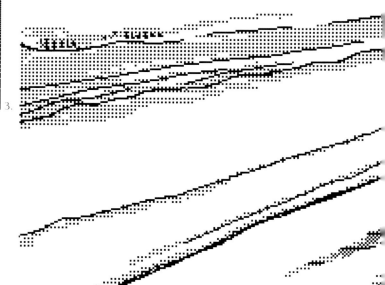

1.

2.

3.

4.

MATTIS
DOVIER
—

1. – 3. WILD BEASTS – GIF NOVEL 4. FEAR AND LOATHING IN PRAGUE

POST REALISM

MATT
ROTA
—

1. & 3. FIRESTONE AND THE WARLORD 2. FREEDOM RIDERS 4. WRONG PATH

POST REALISM

2.

4.

EMIN METE
ERDOĞAN
—

1. AW02 2. B3 3. B4 4. B1

3.

4.

EMIN METE ERDOĞAN | *POST REALISM*

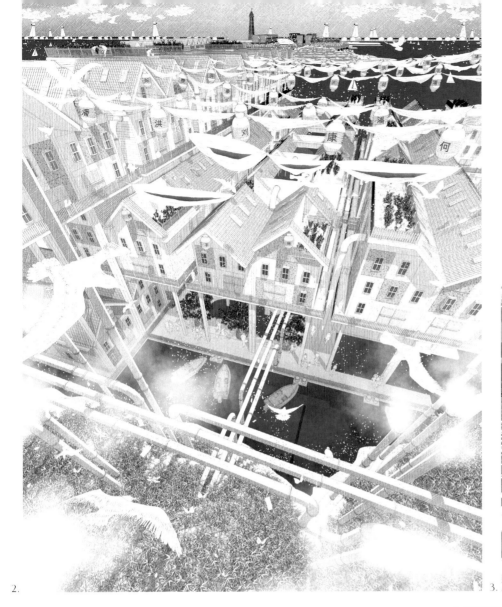

2.

3.

4.

JASON
LAMB
—

FRACKPOOL: 1. THE LEGACY OF BLOOMFIELD FRACKING STATION 2. OFFSHORE COMMUNITIES ROOFTOP GARDENING AND RAINWATER COLLECTION 3. CONSTRUCTING BLOOMFIELD FRACKING STATION 4. THE LEGACY OF FRACKPOOL SUSTAINABLE ENERGY PRODUCTION AND NEW INDUSTRY

CHRISTOPH
NIEMANN
—

PRICE $6.99   **THE**   OCT. 6, 2014

NEW YORKER

2.

3.

1. RAINY DAY 2. & 3. ONE SMALL STEP AT A TIME. 4. & 5. IM KRAFTFELD VON KRAFTWERK

CHRISTOPH NIEMANN | POST REALISM

alpha sound
GmbH
Tel. 030 44 67 910

4.

5.

1. EDGE OF THE WORLD 2. CRAZY LEGS

POST REALISM

1.

2.

JOE
IURATO
—

1.

2.

3.

JÖNS
MELLGREN
—

DR KHAN'S STORY

POST REALISM

4.

5.

MARIO
HUGO
—

1. PHILOPOEMEN 2. UNITED BAMBOO 3. SHOW SOME HEART 4. UNITED BAMBOO 5. RIHANNA UNAPOLOGETIC

POST REALISM

5.

1.

2.

3.

ALANA DEE
HAYNES
—

1 – 3. UNTITLED

POST REALISM

FLORIAN
BAYER
—

1 – 4. DIE HALBE WAHRHEIT

1. SCHIEFE BAHN 2. THE KILLING OF GEMMA 3. TRAVELBOOK PORTUGAL

1.

3.

2.

4.

TIM
LAING
—

1. CHASE 2. MEET 3. HONOUR 4. KAPLA

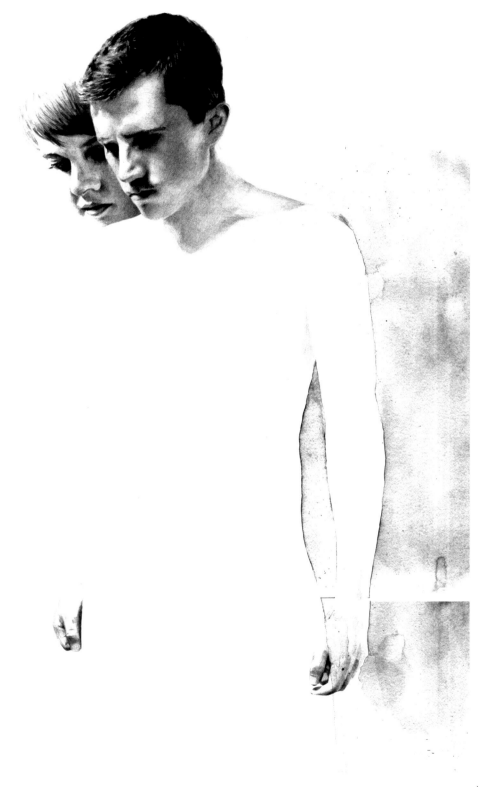

TIM LAING | POST PEALISM

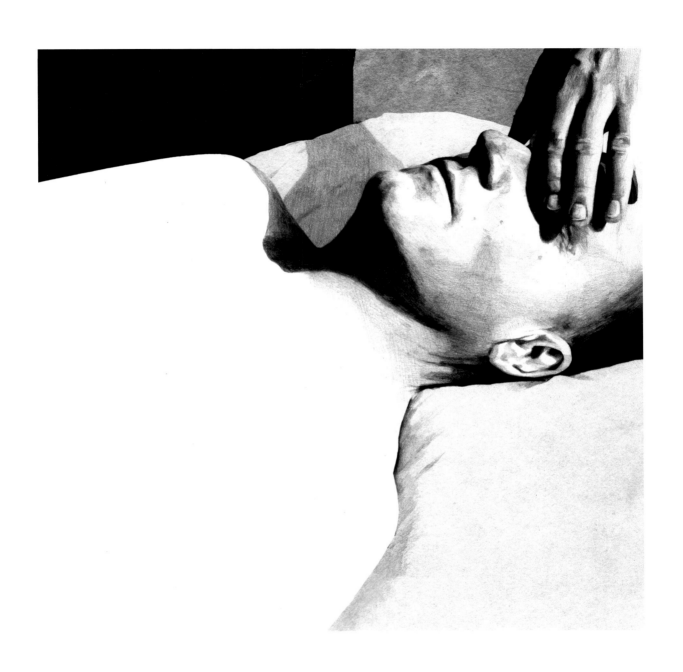

2.

1. C & K 2. MED

1. MIAMI 2. PARIS 3. HOUSES

INFORMATION & GRAPHICS

2.

3.

1.

HATTIE
NEWMAN
—

1. DREAM HOME 1 2. EARTH DAY   2.

1.

1. & 4. INSTALLATION FOR THE QUEEN'S DIAMOND JUBILEE 2. – 5. CHRISTMAS WINDOW INSTALLATION

INFORMATION & GRAPHICS

2.

3.

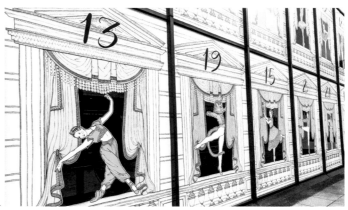

4.

5.

PETER
GRUNDY
—

Stay in touch
with your street lights

CityTouch Lightwave
Remote Lighting Management

1.

Bring light into your
lighting operations

CityTouch Lightpoint
Lighting Asset Management

2.

3.

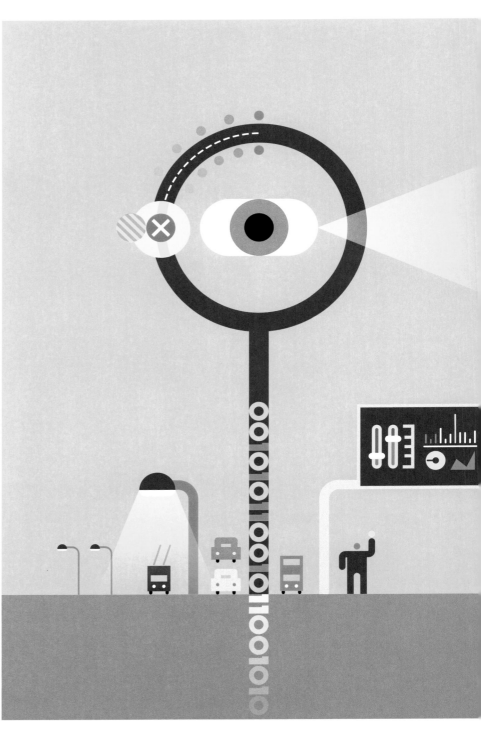

1. – 4. CITYTOUCH LIGHTING COFELY ADVERTISING CAMPAIGN

ROBERT SAMUEL
HANSON
—

1.

2.

3.

4.

1.–3. ILLUSTRATIONS FOR A-Z OF DESIGN – MONOCLE ALPINO NEWSPAPER 4. NEWSWEEK DRUGS

APFEL
ZET
—

1.

2.

3.

1. OVERHEAD TRAFFICWAYS 2. FRESH UP 3. AIR HARBOUR AND TRAIN STATION 4. ALFA ROMEO ANNIVERSARY

4.

1.

JULENE
HARRISON
—

1. THERE IS A LIGHT 2. GO FURTHER

1.

2.

3.

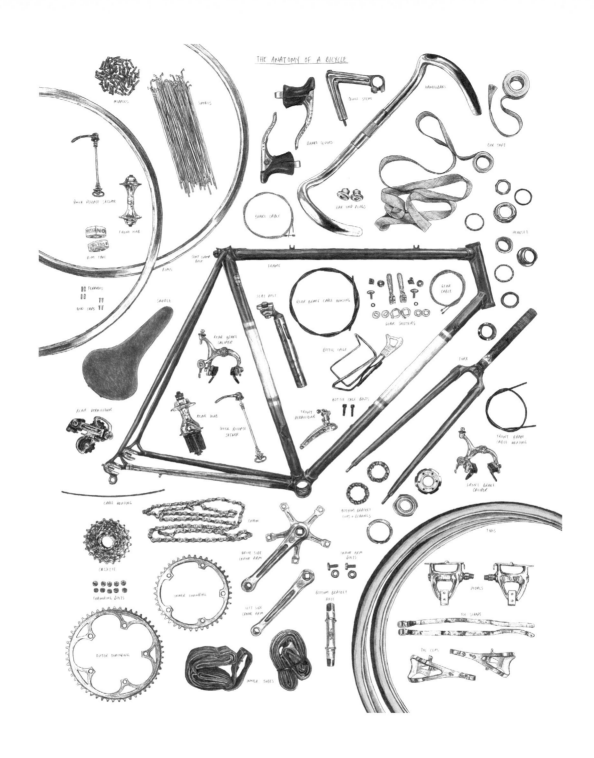

THE ANATOMY OF A BICYCLE

DAVID
SPARSHOTT
—

1. ANATOMY OF A BICYCLE 2. BICYCLE RACE SUPPORT VEHICLES

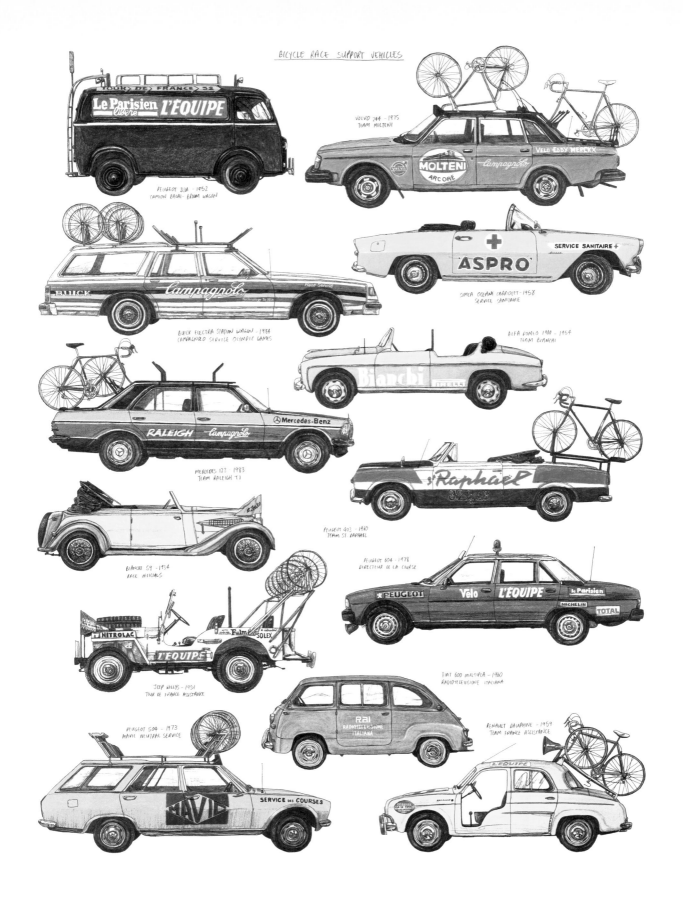

BICYCLE RACE SUPPORT VEHICLES

PEUGEOT D3A - 1952
CAMION BALAI - BROOM WAGON

VOLVO 244 - 1975
TEAM MOLTENI

BUICK ELECTRA STATION WAGON - 1984
CAMPAGNOLO SERVICE OLYMPIC GAMES

SIMCA OCÉANE CABRIOLET - 1958
SERVICE SANITAIRE

ALFA ROMEO 1900 - 1954
TEAM BIANCHI

MERCEDES 123 - 1983
TEAM RALEIGH TI

BIANCHI S9 - 1934
RACE OFFICIALS

PEUGEOT 403 - 1960
TEAM ST RAPHAEL

PEUGEOT 604 - 1978
DIRECTEUR DE LA COURSE

JEEP WILLYS - 1951
TOUR DE FRANCE ASSISTANCE

FIAT 600 MULTIPLA - 1960
RADIOTELEVISIONE ITALIANA

PEUGEOT 504 - 1973
MAVIC NEUTRAL SERVICE

RENAULT DAUPHINE - 1959
TEAM FRANCE ASSISTANCE

2.

MISTER
MOURAO
—

1. NEW YORK PERCEPTIONS 2. NEW YORK PERCEPTIONS I 3. PERCEPTIONS OF CENTRAL PARK

ANTOINE
CORBINEAU
—

1. URSULINE ACADEMY OF DALLAS 2. WINTER IS COMING

INFORMATION & GRAPHICS

Antoine Corlineau

A MAP OF PARIS

ANTOINE CORBINEAU | INFORMATION & GRAPHICS

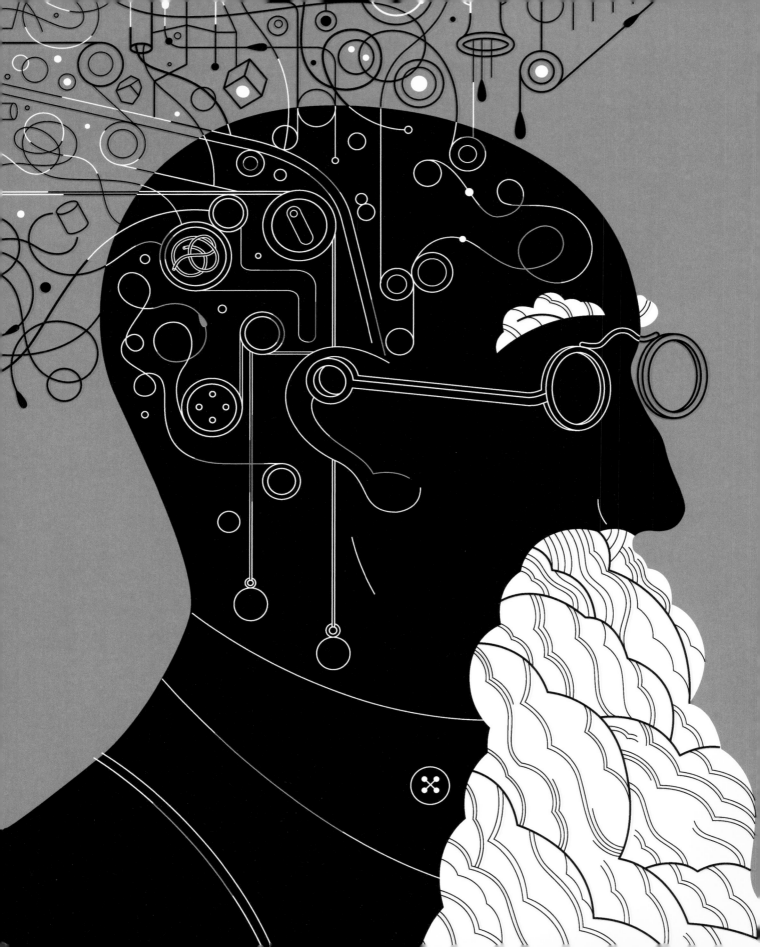

2.

HARRY
CAMPBELL
—

1. MASTERS 2. BIRD CAGE

1.

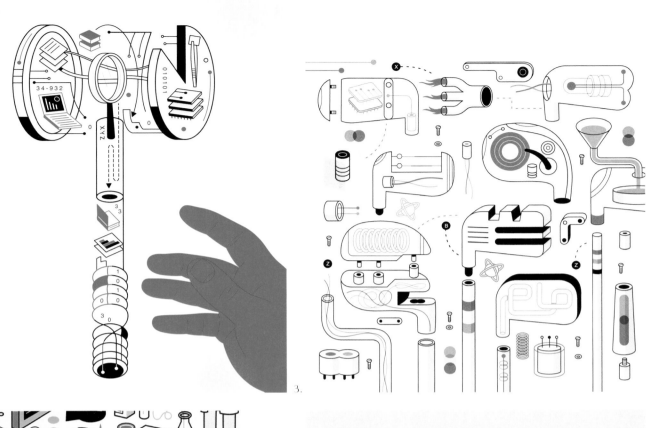

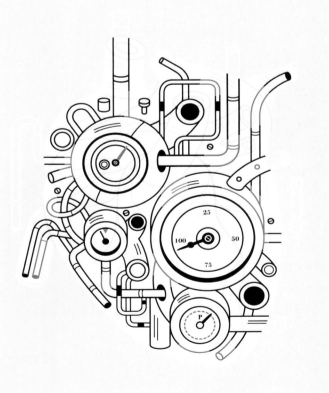

1. INDUSTRIAL HAND 2. GAVEL 3. CLUB VARIETY 4. RECIPE FOR HEALTH 5. MECHANICAL HEART

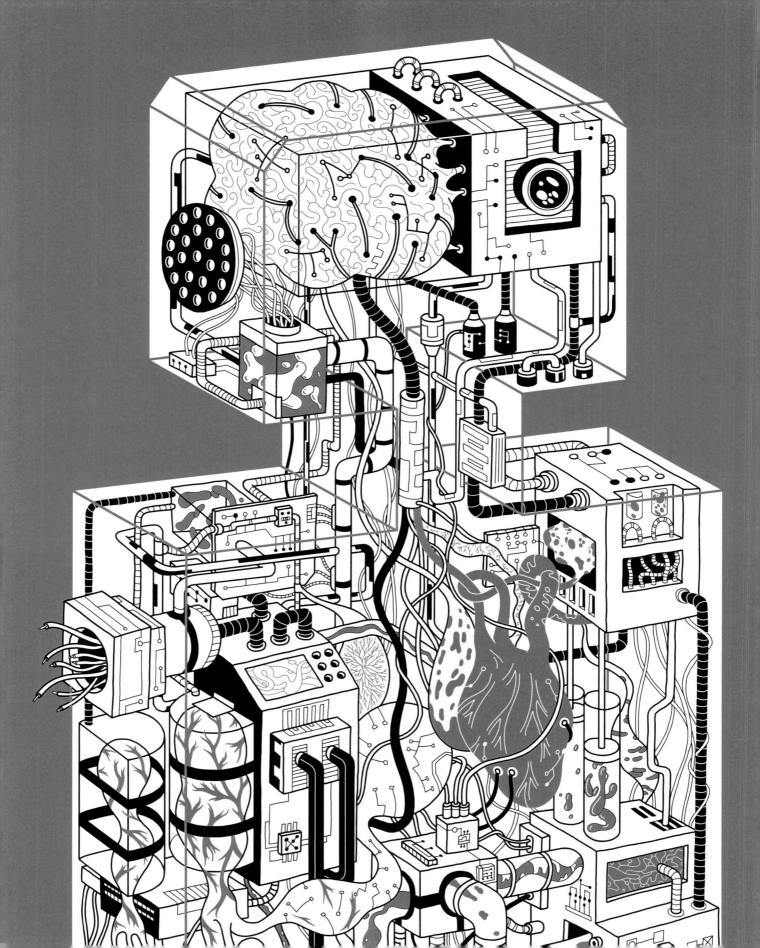

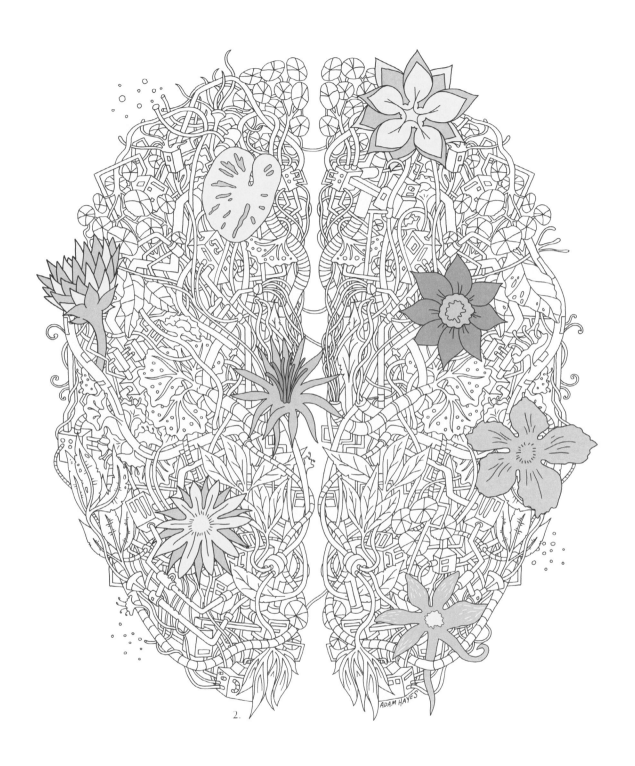

ADAM
HAYES
—

1. MAN MACHINE 2. A BEAUTIFUL MIND

1.

MY HEART.
(a diagram)

CAKE
TACOS
BACON
YOU

MIKE
LOWERY
—

1. MY TEXAS DO BEFORE I DIE LIST 2. YOU HAVE (MOST OF) MY HEART 3. MY TATTOOS

2.

I ♥ HAND DRAWN TYPE

MIKE LOWERY ILLUSTRATION

TACOS

MIKELOWERY.COM

3.

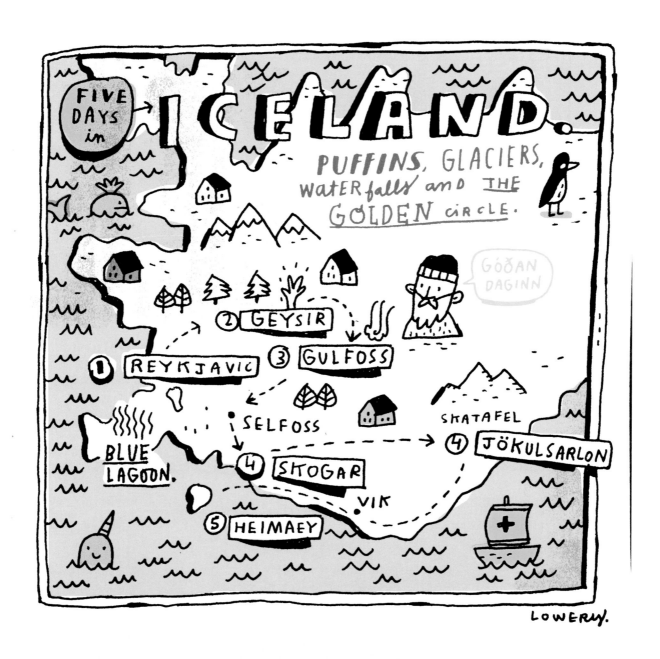

1. A FEW DAYS IN ICELAND 2. HOME IS WHEREVER I'M WITH YOU

2.

COMA DEEP

BRIGID DEACON

BRIGID
DEACON
—

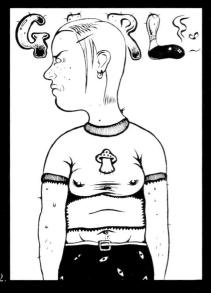

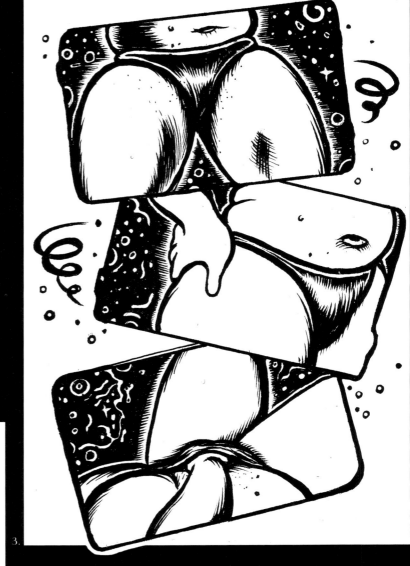

2.

3.

1.

5.

1.

3.

2.

LAYZELL
BROS
—
1. KIDS RUNNING WILD 2. A3 PRINT "CITY LIVING" 3. RED WHITE BLACK 4. ANIMATED GIF

1.

2.

RAYMOND
LEMSTRA
—

1.– 2. COVER AND JUMP PAGE – THE NEW YORK TIMES SUNDAY REVIEW

POP & REBELLION

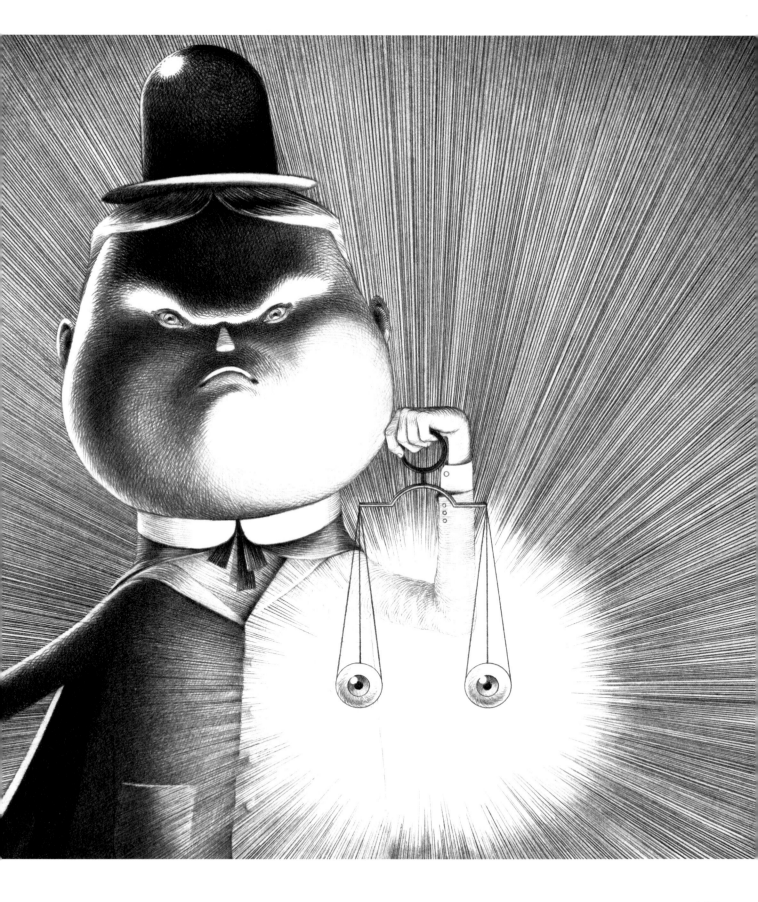

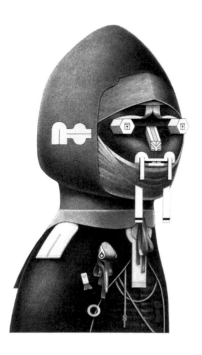

BIG MOTHER
- RAYMOND ••••• LEMSTRA -

NOBROW PRESS LONDON

1.

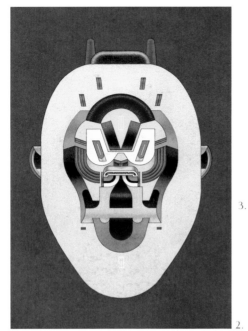

3.

2.

1. COLETTE 2. ASAP MOB 3. BIG MOTHER 4 4. THE JAUNT SEOUL

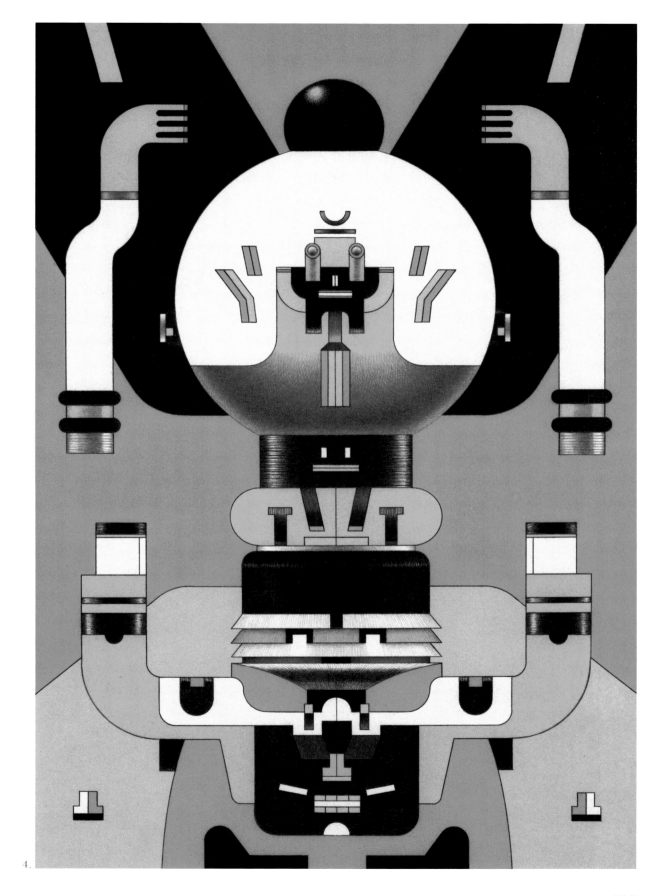

4.

BMD
DESIGN
—

1.

2.

BELLA MATRIBUS DETESTAS: 1. APERTO_LIBRO 2. CLUB BELLA 3. TABLIERS BELLA

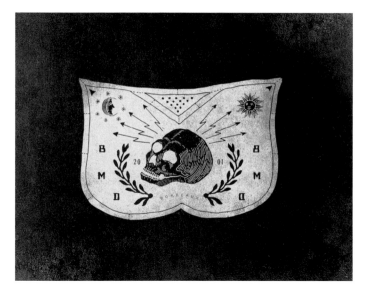

3.

KYLE
PLATTS
—

1. HOW TO ACCEPT FUTURE BILLIONAIRES TO HARVARD 2. NICE WRITING 3. ISSUE 3 COVER 4. GUIDE TO SUMMER

5.

5. P. NEWBOLD COLLABORATION

RICK
BERKELMANS
—

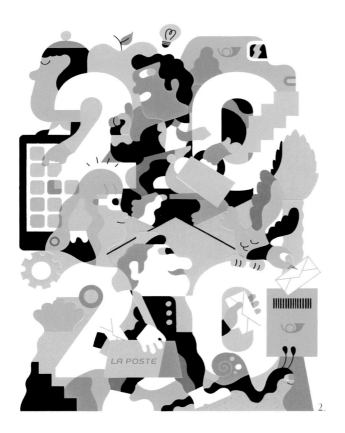

1. SAINT HUBERT 2. OTHERWISE 3. DOWNSTREAM 4. THE FOX HUNT

Parterre de Rois

PDR

#02/ABSENT

1.

#03 REBELLION

NUMÉRO TRE / 2015 // Euro 18.00 / USD 20.00 / GBP 16.00

2.

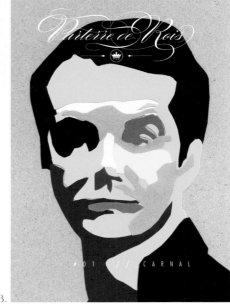

#01 // CARNAL

3.

PARTERRE
DE ROIS
—

1. ABSENT RIVER 2. REBEL LYDIA 3. CARNAL JACK

POP & REBELLION

3.

SHAN
JIANG
—

1. SPACE ODYSSEY 2. MOONPHASE 3. DROWNING MAN

POP & REBELLION

2.

3.

4.

EERO
LAMPINEN
—

1. INSECT COLLECTOR 2. DEPLETION 3. FEEDING HOUR 4. SEEDS

BIANCA
BAGNARELLI
—

1. LA BANDE DESTINÉE 2. DELEBILE – WORK 3. LOVE, DEATH AND SPAGHETTI – THE NEW YORK TIMES

3.

OLIMPIA
ZAGNOLI
—

1.

2.

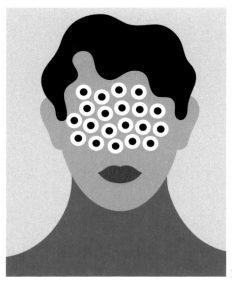

3.

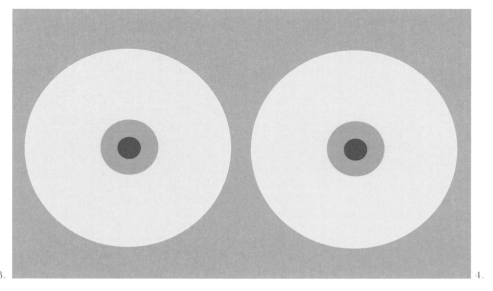

4.

1. TWENTIETH ANNIVERSARY OF VITA MAGAZINE 2. THE SUN – THE NEW YORK TIMES SUNDAY REVIEW 3. "KEEP THE THOUGHT IN MOTION" – INTERNAZIONALE ABOUT THE PHILOSOPHY OF SLAVOJ ŽIŽEK 4. COVER FOR "TROPICO DEL CAPRICORNO" – FELTRINELLI

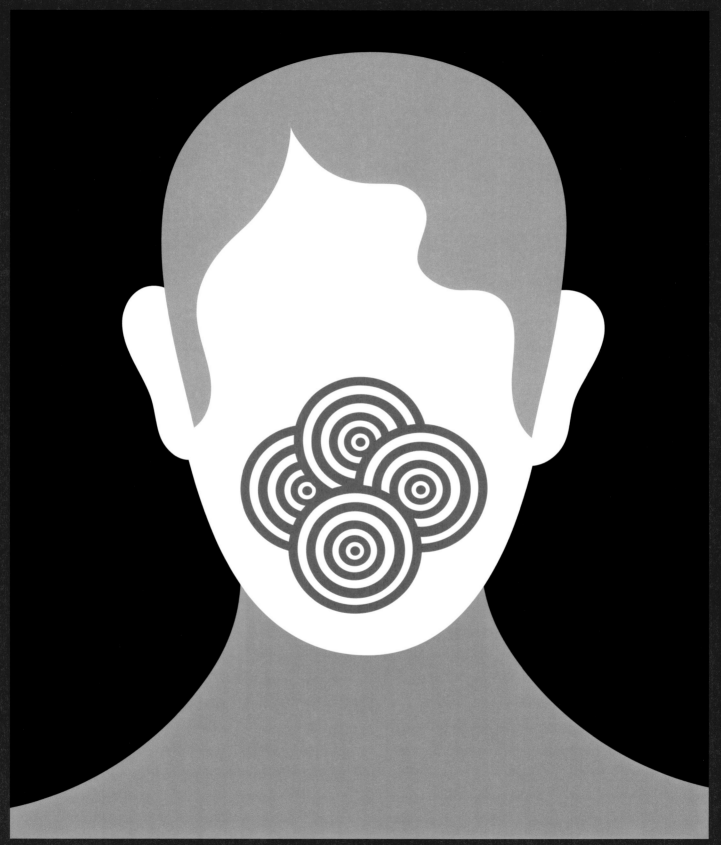

5. "WHY SAVE A LANGUAGE?" – THE NEW YORK TIMES

2.

1.

3.

1. "C'ERA UNA VOLTA L'INFANZIA" – LA REPUBBLICA 2. FINDING PEACE THROUGH FRIENDSHIP – THE NEW YORK TIMES SUNDAY REVIEW

3. UNTITLED 4. DON'T WORRY, GET BOTOX – THE NEW YORK TIMES SUNDAY REVIEW

OLIMPIA ZAGNOLI | POP & REBELLION   179

1.

LIZ
MEYER
—

1. RACHAEL 2. SAD GIRL 3. RUNNER 4. EVOLUTION OF WRITING TOOLS

TONI
HALONEN
—

1. KINGFISHERS 2. OBSERVER

2.

2.

3.

4.

5.

1. KENZOPEDIA 2. BEACH 3. PORTRAIT OF OSMA HARVILAHTI 4. MODULOR 5. LGC BILLBOARD FOR IT'S NICE THAT'S LONDON GRAPHIC CENTRE

1. ODALISQUE 2. TRAVEL + LEISURE

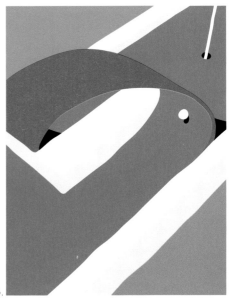

3. KENZOPEDIA – KENZO ROYAL BLUE 4. POETRY JAM 5. TRENDI MAGAZINE 6. MINIGOLF – SPORTS BEYONDERGROUND HELSINKI 2014 EXHIBITION

RYU
ITADANI
—

1. INTERSECT BY LEXUS 2. SOUVENIR FROM TOKYO

2.

3. MONOCLE 4. INTERSECT BY LEXUS

1. ADONIS 2. HANGOVER CHIC 4-EVER

POP & REBELLION

1.

SARA
ANDREASSON
—

2.

1. & 3. HANGOVER CHIC 4-EVER 2. & 4. WHITE NOISE 5. INTERNATIONAL WOMEN'S DAY

SARA ANDREASSON | POP & REBELLION

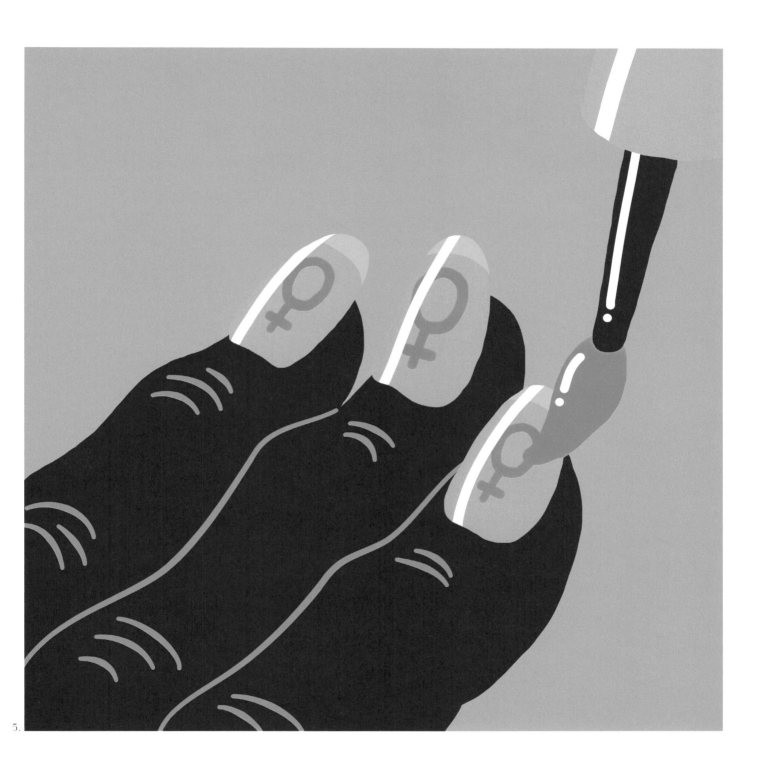

5.

ELENI
KALORKOTI
—

1. JULY 2. BATTERSEA PARK 3. BATHING 4. CLARA SCHUMANN

196 THE CLASSICS

2.

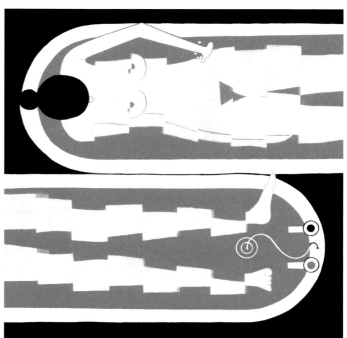

3.

4.

THE CLASSICS

1.

DANIEL
CLARKE
–

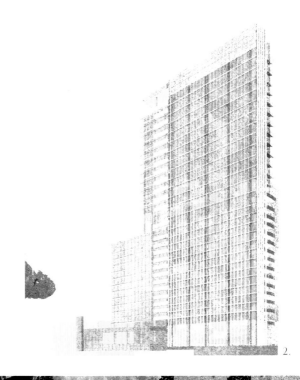

EDITORIAL WORKS: 1. PERSONAL WORK 2. & 3. WALLPAPER MAGAZINE 4. SMITH JOURNAL 5. CASA CAVIA FACADE

DANIEL CLARKE | THE CLASSICS

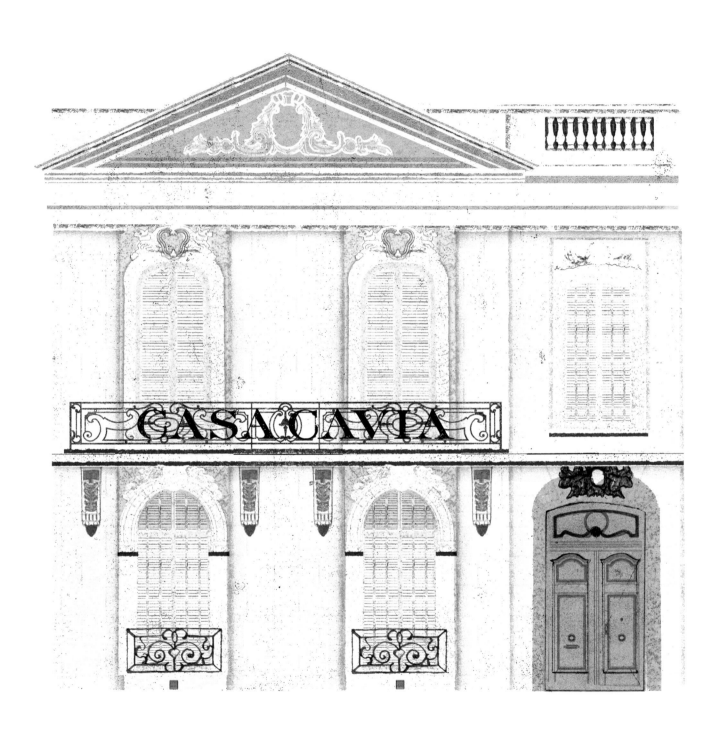

5.

DELPHINE
LEBOURGEOIS
—

1. & 2. FALL

THE CLASSICS

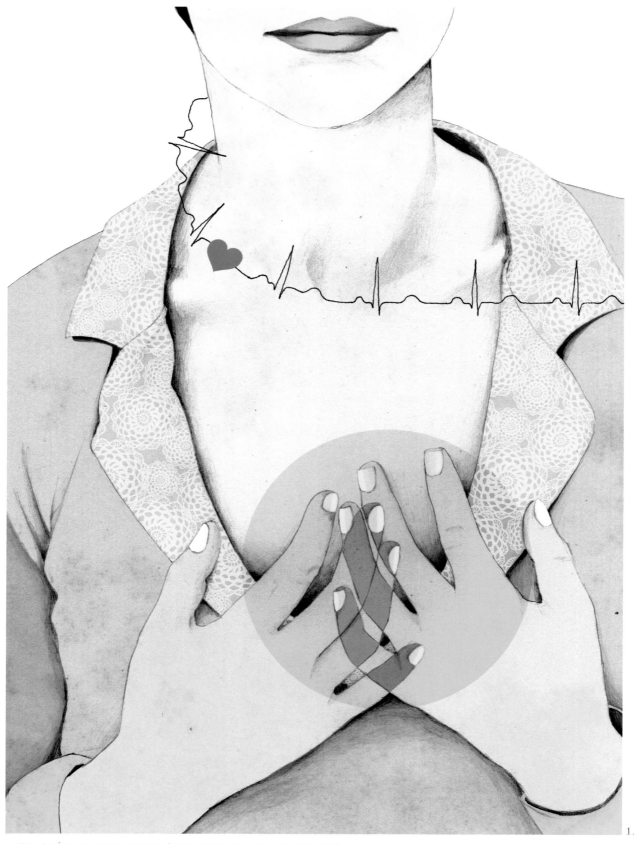

1. TOUCHÉES EN PLEIN COEUR ("TOUCHED IN THE VERY HEART")

DELPHINE LEBOURGEOIS | THE CLASSICS

2.

3.

2. THE FUTURE OF LATIN AND ANCIENT GREEK IN FRENCH EDUCATION 3. "DE LA SOUFFRANCE" (ABORTION LAWS IN FRANCE)

DELPHINE LEBOURGEOIS | THE CLASSICS

PATRICK
MORGAN
—

1.

2.

325 LEXINGTON PROJECT

3.

1. MAD MAX – FURY ROAD 2. IMAGINING ALEXANDRE JOLLIEN STUDYING ZAZEN IN SEOUL AND FINDING BALANCE

THE CLASSICS

LUCILLE
CLERC
–

3. IMAGINARY PORTRAIT OF ALEXANDRE JOLLIEN WHO NOW LIVES IN SEOUL

1.

ANNA & ELENA
BALBUSSO
—

1. A GUT FEELING 2. & 4. EUGENE ONEGIN BY ALEXANDER PUSHKIN 3. PRIDE AND PREJUDICE BY JANE AUSTEN

2.

3.

4.

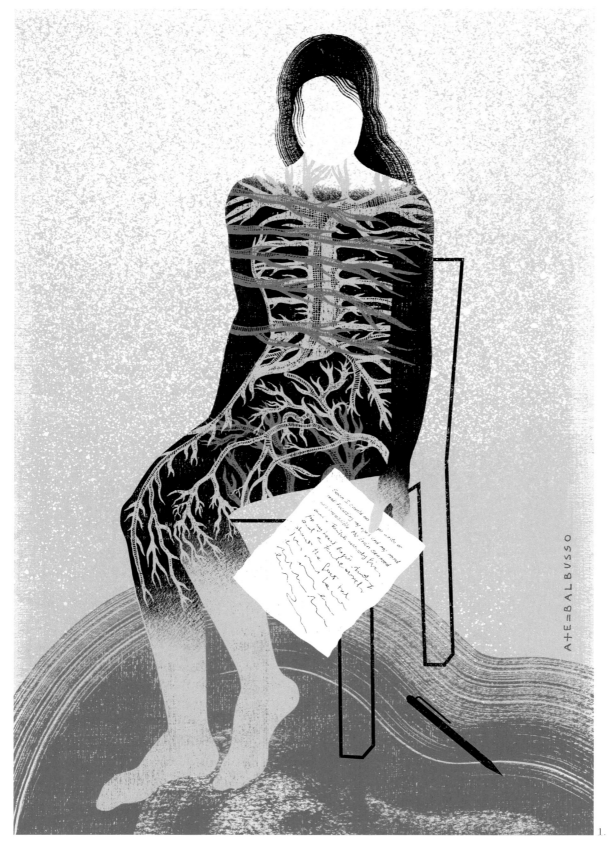

1. AUTOIMMUNE DISEASE 2. LA PETITE CHIPETTE – ISOLATION

ANNA & ELENA BALBUSSO | THE CLASSICS

2.

1.

MICHAEL
MORGENSTERN
—

1. CHINA, OLYMPIC VICTIM? 2. TIGER CUBS VS PRECIOUS LAMBS 3. THE IMPORTANCE OF BEING INSINCERE

214

2.

3.

4.

4. AND THEN THEY CAME FOP THE JUDGES. FOP THE ECONOMIST MAGAZINE

1. GETTING IN THE WAY 2. ON THE ANTLERS OF A DILEMMA 3. BIRTHDAY BLUES 4. ON THE DEFENSIVE 5. BLEAK HOUSE
6. A HALF-PIKE UP THE NOSTRIL 7. DOES THE ELEPHANT DANCE? 8. FORCE MAJEURE

MICHAEL MORGENSTERN | THE CLASSICS

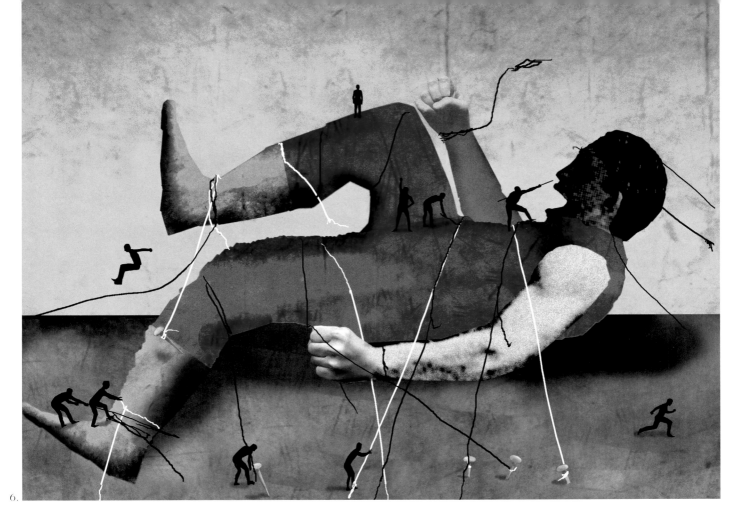

6.

7.

8.

1. VALE OF TEARS 2. THE GREAT WAVE 3. AN EXERCISE IN FERTILITY

MICHAEL MORGENSTERN | THE CLASSICS

ANA
JUAN
—

LA ISLA BAJA EL MAP: 1. SNOWHITE 2. JOE TURNER 3. OTRA VUELTA DE TUERCA 4. DPI

LA ISLA BAJA EL MAR: 1. WITCH I, HAENSEL & GRETEL 2. ALLENDE   2.

2.

3.

4.

ANDREA
VENTURA
—

1. ELSA MORANTE 2. RALPH FIENNES AS HAMLET 3. CURTIS MAYFIELD 4. LOUIS ARMSTRONG

1. MAN IN BLUE 2. KOFI ANNAN 3. MARIE DE VILLEPIN 4. AMOS OZ 5. SEAN CONNERY AS 007

1.

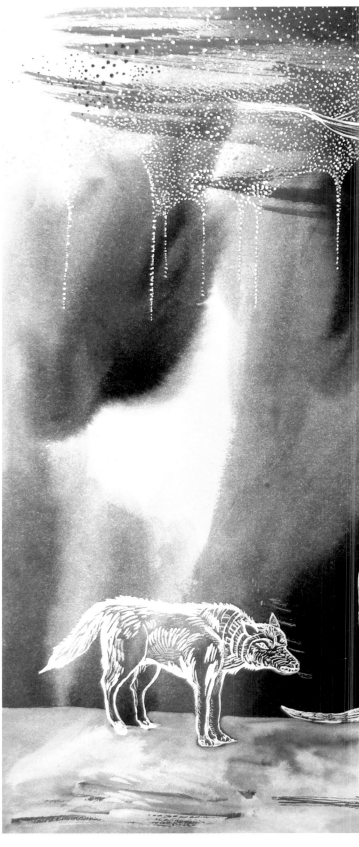

2.

KAREN
BARBOUR
—

1. EYE CURTAIN 2. GIRL IN FOREST

THE CLASSICS

1. YOU GOT THE DEVIL IN YOU 2. DAISY 3. GIRL WITH A ROCK ON HER HEAD 4. GIRL AND BEAR

2.

3.

4.

THE CLASSICS

1.

KEITH
NEGLEY
—

3.

1. HEALTH 2. BATTLE 3. SUICIDE 4. HOAPDER

2.

3.

4.

EMMA
LÖFSTRÖM
–

1. & 2. ILLUSTRATION INSPIRED BY JOHN GALLIANO FOR 1 GRANARY MAGAZINE 3. MINNEN FRÅN NOPP. ILLUSTRATION BASED ON GRIMM'S FAIRY TALES 4. PUSS IN BOOTS, ILLUSTRATION BASED ON GRIMM'S FAIRY TALES

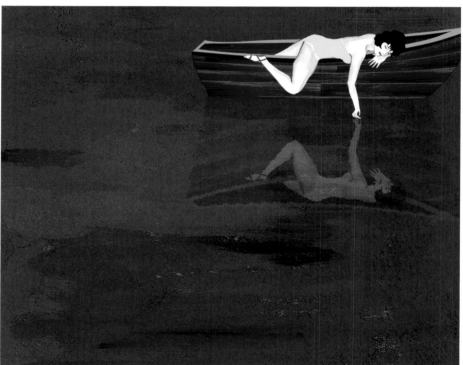

GIGI ROSE
GRAY
—

1. PALMS 2. ON THE DOCK 3. ON THE BOAT 4. TO FERNAND

THE CLASSICS

1. LOOKING UP 2. SKYSCRAPERS 3. 3 WOMEN

GIGI ROSE GRAY | THE CLASSICS

2.

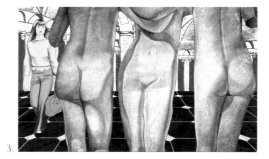

1.

3.

DAVID
DORAN
—

1. WOMEN IN WINEMAKING

THE CLASSICS

2. THE SUSTAINABILITY OF SELF-BUILT HOUSES 3. THE WEALTH DIVIDE IN NEW DELHI, INDIA 4. MAN AT THE HELM

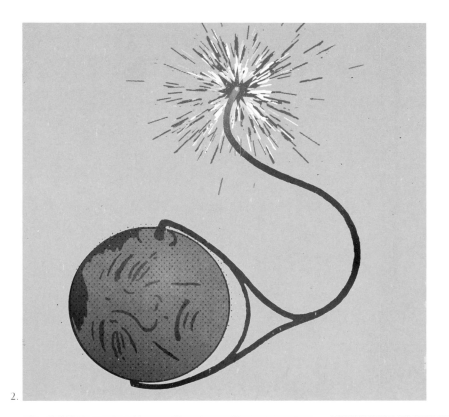

3.

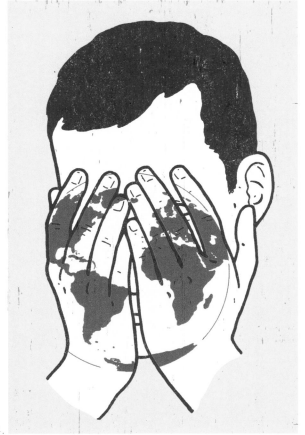

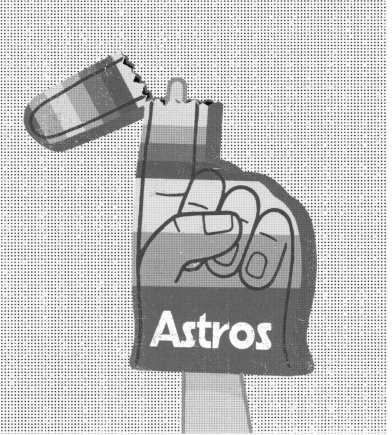

4.   5.

1. CRIMINAL RECORD 2. DOCTOR BURNOUT 3. COMING CLEAN 4. JUDGE 5. NUMBER ONE

1. BEST GAME 2. R & D IDEAS

DAN PAGE | THE CLASSICS

KINDRED
STUDIO
—

1. ALPHABETICA 2. CLOUDSOURCING 3. AUSTRALIAN TOUR POSTER 4. BOSS MAGAZINE

4.

1.

1. INSIDER GUIDES 2. & 3. OLIVER GRAND

2.

3.

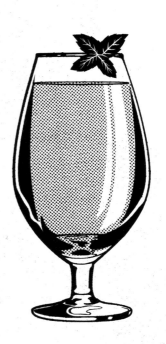

1.

1. MR BLACK 2. & 5. HOW THE WORLD ENDS 3. ART VS SCIENCE 4. WIN/LOSE

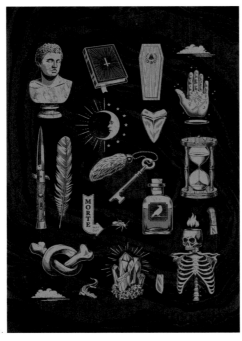

MATTHEW
WOODSON
—

1. THE JOY OF SOLDEPING 2. ALBUQUEPQUE

THE CLASSICS

2.

1. THE BREAK-IN ARTIST 2. THE COMPLICATED TRUTH ABOUT CHILDREN AND DROWNING 3. MAGNIFIED
4. JAMES "WHITEY" BULGER & CATHERINE GREIG'S STORY

JEFFREY
EVERETT
—

1. GHOSTS OF THE BOARDWALK 2. FRANK TURNER AT THE 9:30 CLUB

THE CLASSICS

2.

SHOUT

—

1. FOREIGN LANGUAGE GAY MOVIES

2. PRIVACY WAR 3. YOU DON'T KNOW WHAT LOVE IS – RAY CARVER BOOK COVER 4. SECRET SERVICE

1.   2.

3.

1. AMERICA ALTOGETHER 2. PLACES 3. GENERATION GAP 4. BOOK REVIEW

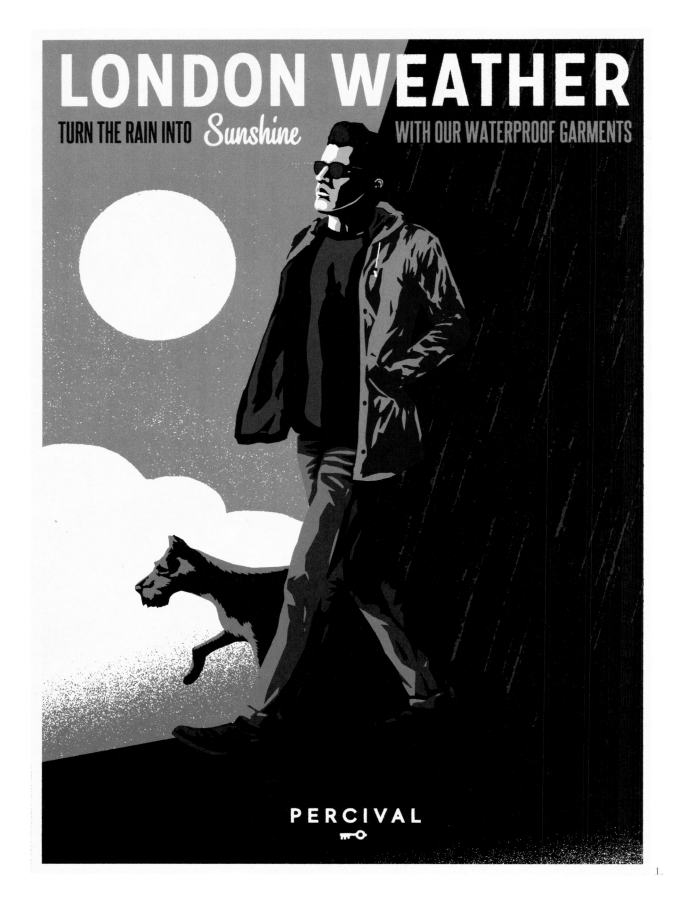

3.

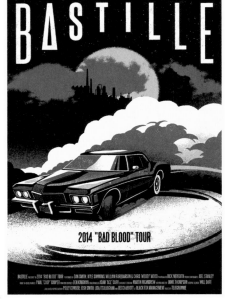

2.

4.

TELEGRAMME
PAPER CO.
—

1. & 3. PERCIVAL POSTER CAMPAIGN 2. & 4. BASTILLE GIG POSTERS

POSTER BY TELEGRAMME

3.

2.

4.

5.

1. – 5. SOHO HOUSE WINTER POSTERS

1.

TOM
HAUGOMAT
—

1. UNTIL FOREVER RUNS OUT – POPSHOT MAGAZINE 2. BULLY APPS – PROTEIN MAGAZINE

THE CLASSICS

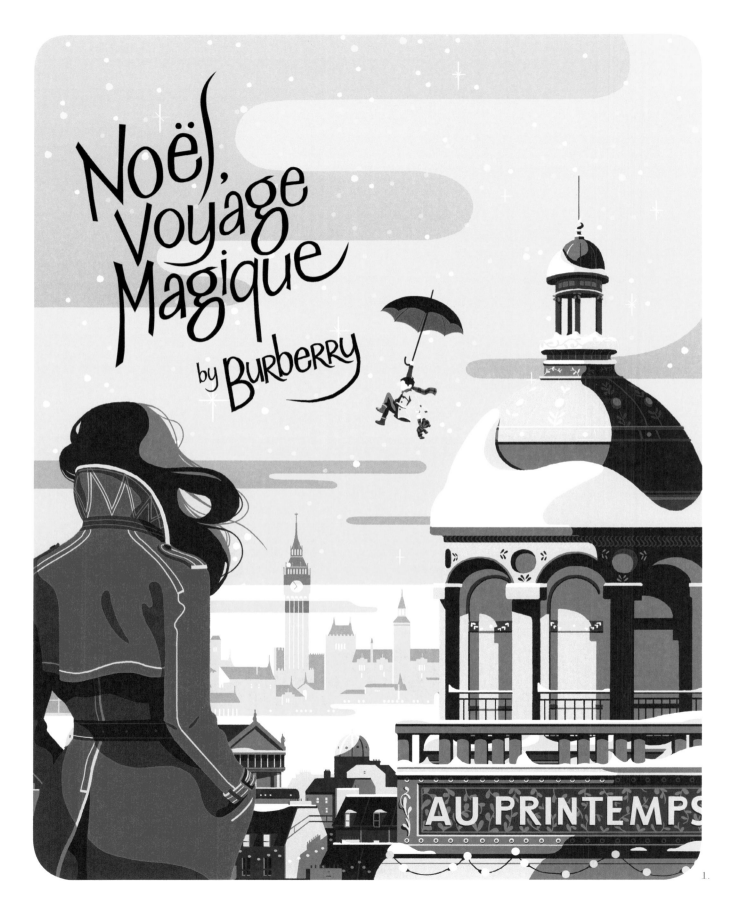

1.–4. PRINTEMPS PORTRAIT – BURBERRY CHRISTMAS WINDOWS

MADS
BERG
—

YOGHURT *fra*

Hansens

MEJERI

1.

2.

3.

4.

1. BORNHOLM 15 2. HANSEN'S YOGHURT 3. EL HIERRO – PLAYA DEL VERODAL 4. L'OCCITANE – LE JARDIN D'HIVER
5. ENGADINA – AMAPO ALPINO

5.

1. BOTTEGA VENETA 2. EL HIERRO - JINAMA

EL HIERRO

MIRADOR DE JINAMA HELLOCANARYISLANDS.COM

2.

1.

2.

3.

4.

JEFFREY
EVERETT
—

PORTRAIT SERIES: 1. DON DRAPER 2. HENRY ROLLINS 3. JOE STRUMMER 4. BOB DYLAN 5. JOHNNY CASH

THE CLASSICS

5.

GREETINGS FROM
LOS ANGELES

1.

THOMAS
DANTHONY
—

1. & 2. GREETINGS FROM LOS ANGELES

GREETINGS FROM
LOS ANGELES

GREETINGS FROM
LOS ANGELES

GREETINGS FROM
LOS ANGELES

GREETINGS FROM
LOS ANGELES

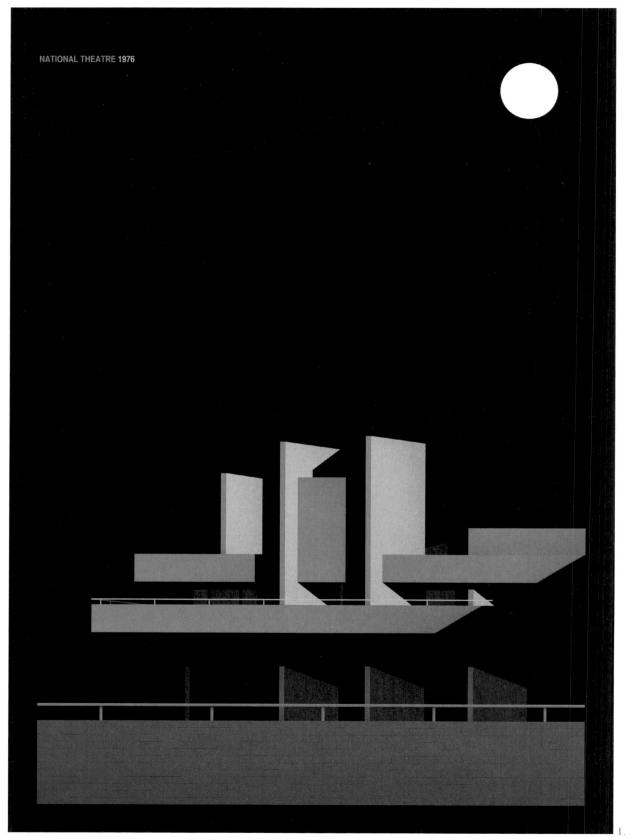

NATIONAL THEATRE 1976

1. & 2. BRUTALISM

THOMAS DANTHONY | THE CLASSICS

TRELLICK TOWER **1972**

2.

THOMAS DANTHONY | THE CLASSICS

JULIA
GEISER
—

COLLAGE

1. BAMBI 2. A SWAN LAKE 3. & 4. MONA II 5. MONA I

5.

PAUL
REILLY
—

PIETER: 1. PIHANNA 2. ERYKAH 3. MICHAEL 4. AALIYAH

290   COLLAGE

2.

3.

4.

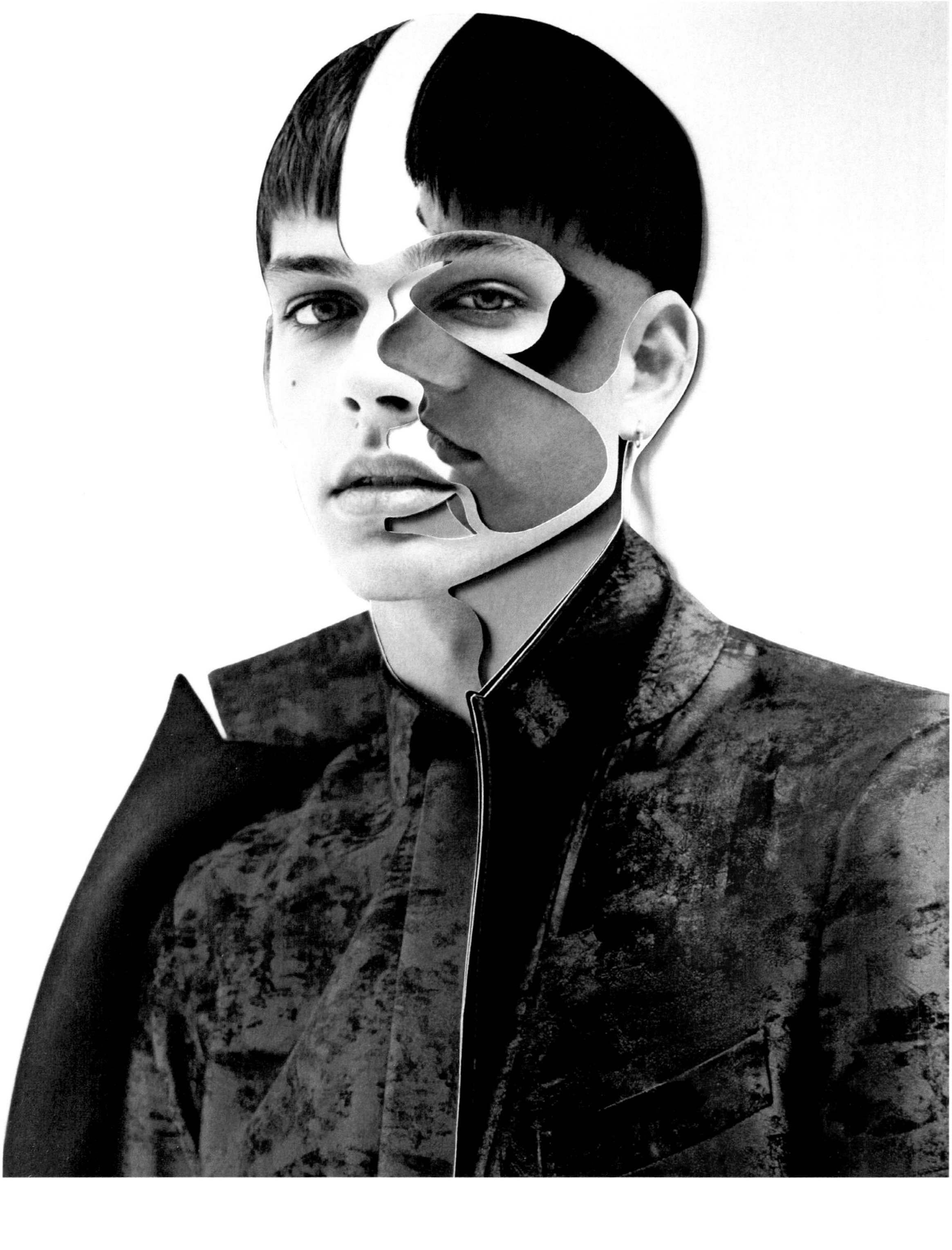

1.

DAMIEN
BLOTTIERE

—

1. & 2. "THE SHAPE OF THINGS TO COME"

1. & 2. "THE SHAPE OF THINGS TO COME"

DAMIEN BLOTTIERE | COLLAGE

2.

LOLA
DUPRÉ
—

1. MINA 2. JOHN FRENCH WITH HASSELBLAD

COLLAGE

2.

COLLAGE

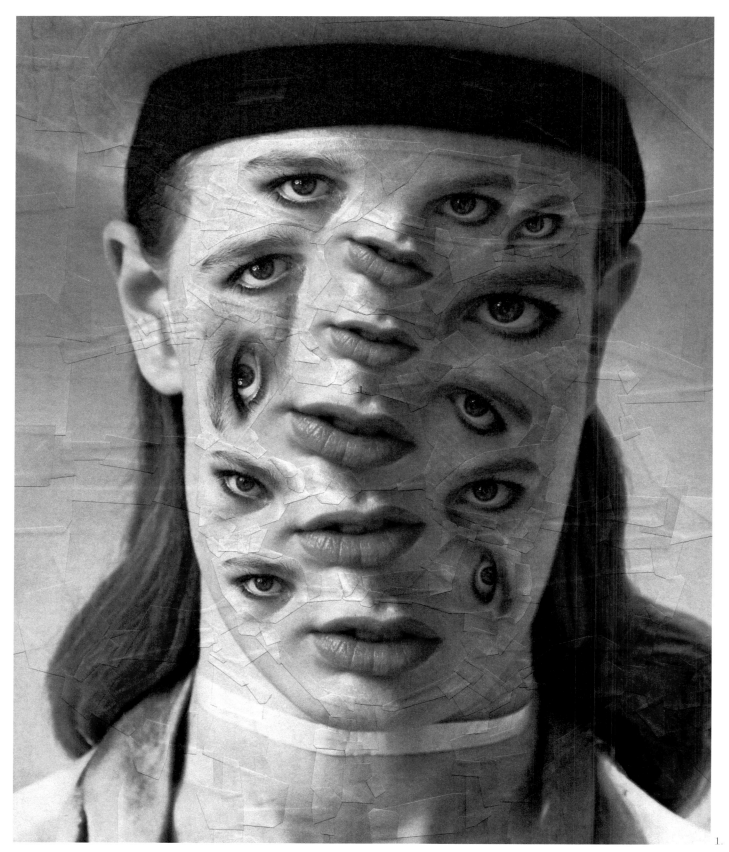

1. UNTITLED WITH WILLIAM KANO

LOLA DUPRÉ | COLLAGE

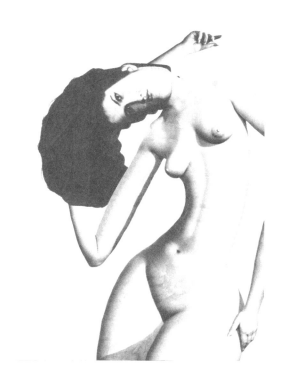

2. UNTITLED WITH WILLIAM KANO 3. CHIC DESNUDA 4. UNTITLED WITH JONATHAN WAITER

1. – 4. UNTITLED WITH WILLIAM KANO

Zezon lit.

S.A.I.R.
IL PRINCIPE D. LUIGI BORBONE
Conte d'Aquila
VICE AMMIRACLIO
74

1.

COLLAGE

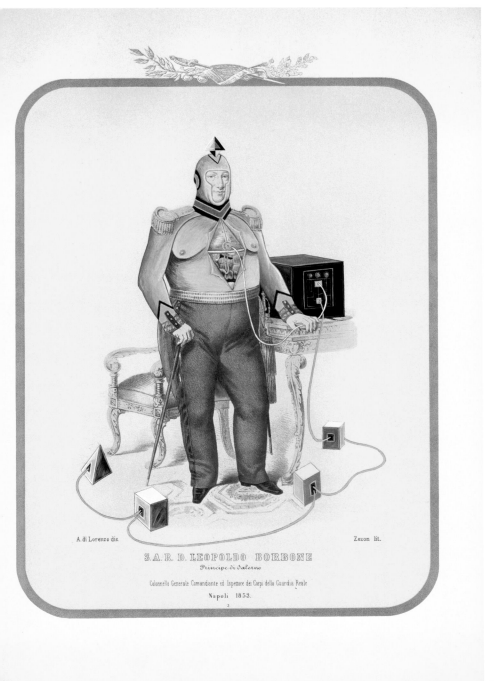

A. di Lorenzo dis.   Zezon lit.

S.A.R. D. LEOPOLDO BORBONE
Principe di Salerno

Colonnello Generale Comandante ed Ispettore dei Corpi della Guardia Reale

Napoli 1853.

2.

3.

MIGUEL ANGEL
VALDIVIA
—

1. ICÔNES D'UN NOUVEL OPDPE MONDIAL N.3 2. ICÔNES D'UN NOUVEL OPDPE MONDIAL N.1
3. ICÔNES D'UN NOUVEL OPDPE MONDIAL N.2

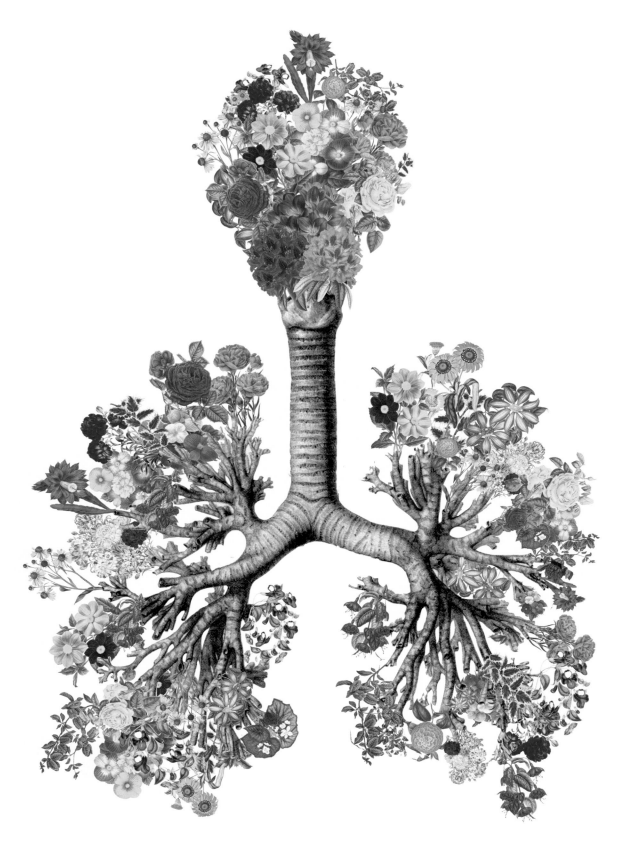

COLLAGE

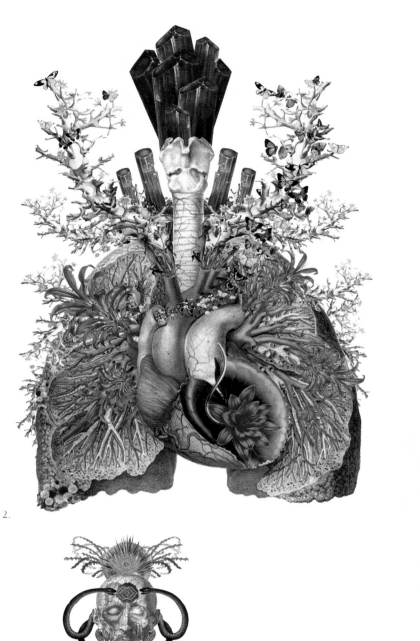

BEDELGEUSE

–

2.

3.   4.

ANATOMICAL COLLAGE: 1. JUST BREATHE 2. ADOPE 3. CHAKRAS 4. BALL AND CHAIN

ANATOMICAL COLLAGE: 1. FEELING FLUTTERY 2. INHALE LIFE – EXHALE LOVE 3. ANATOMY OF A FEMALE ORGASM 4. GROW
5. OUTREACHED

JULIEN
PACAUD
—

1. SCIENCE-FICTION 2. "INTERNET: EVERYTHING GOES!" 3. CITIZEN K – RUSSIAN FURNITURE #2

COLLAGE

Деталь вверху справа регулируе
рата (внизу справа), между у
нагнетающего кровь в сердце
давления в сосудах; та же сам
тывает сердцебиение и давление

1. THE SUMMER OF 2011 SONGS: JULEE CRUISE – "FALLING" 2. SURFERS / TRADERS 3. "NEO GORUOUS" 4. THE RELIVE BOX
5. ARTICLE ABOUT DOMINIQUE A'S SONG

1.

3.

2.

4.

5.

1. PECOPD COVEPS 2. PPOUST/ FPEUD 3. FPENCH PPESIDENT FPANÇOIS HOLLANDE AND HIS COUNSELOP BEPNAPD POIGNANT
4. EVENING IN "THE WOPKSHOP OF HAPPINESS" 5. THE NEW PPINTEPS 6. HOPOSCOPE OPENEP

1.

PETER
HORVATH
—

1. TURN LEFT AT MARS 2. IN SEARCH OF GREENER PASTURES

COLLAGE

1. THE CENSORS 2. THE HITCHHIKERS 3. WISH YOU WERE HERE 4. THE JAVELIN THROWER 5. THE FACELIFT

1. URBAN EMBRACE 2. THE DIVER 3. THE SELFIE 4. THE SMOKER 5. GALAXY GIRL

2.

MAT
MAITLAND
—

1. MICHAEL JACKSON 2. MICHAEL JACKSON – "XSCAPE" ALBUM COVER

2.

3.

4.

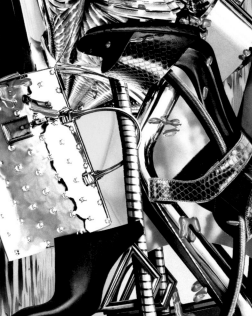

5.

1. & 2. HERO MAGAZINE 3. INTERVIEW RUSSIA / MAGAZINE EDITORIAL 4. HUNTER ORIGINAL SS15 CAMPAIGN FILM / STILLS
5. PLEASE MAGAZINE, PARIS

1.

2.

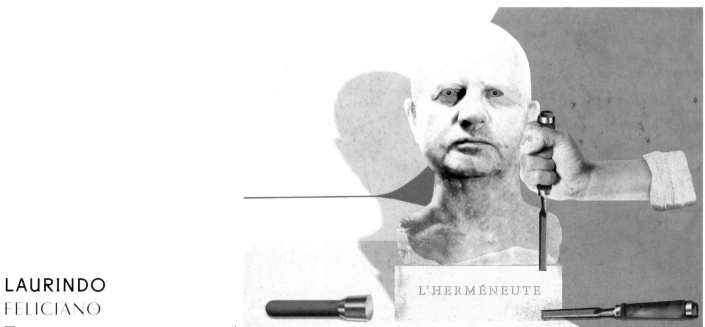

LAURINDO
FELICIANO
—

3.

1. RECIPE I 2. EN 1848 DARWIN SE PEND À MALVERN 3. NETWORK CONNECTIONS

1. FABRICATION SERIES 2. ON THE ROAD 3. SHE'S UNIVERSAL 4. NETWORK CONNECTIONS 5. ALL I LOVED

LAURINDO FELICIANO | COLLAGE

2.

3.

4.

5.

2.

3.

1.

1. ON THE ROAD 2. & 3. FOOTBALL SERIES 4. FABRICATION SERIES

LAURINDO FELICIANO | COLLAGE

1. HOW TO MAKE A DRILL WITH A SHARPENER 2. À TOUS CEUX QUI 3. SWITZERLAND 4. PLAY THE MOVIE

LAURINDO FELICIANO | COLLAGE

MOSTRA
PLAY
THE
MOVIE

5.

1.

2.

3.

1. – 4. SPACEWAPP

4.

MIREILLE
FAUCHON
—

ALMOST

HUMAN

1.

2.

QUENTIN
JONES
—
1. ALMOST HUMAN 2. ADULT SERIES

1.

2.

one must be a Woman Manly

2.

SHONAGH
RAE
—

1. THE NEW REPUBLIC BY LIONEL SHRIVER BOOK REVIEW 2. BRAVE NEW WORLD ALDOUS HUXLEY 3. SECRETS AND LIES

COLLAGE

4.

4. SHOPT STOPY

1. SERENA WILLIAMS PORTRAIT 2. HONOUR BY ELIF SHAFAK

SHONAGH RAE | COLLAGE

1.

2.

3.

MARTIN
O'NEILL
—

4.

5.

6.

1. – 6. BETTINE LE BEAU – A LUCKY GIRL

1. – 4. INTERNATIONAL FASHION SHOWCASE 2015

JAMES
DAWE
—

2.

3.

4.

1.

2.

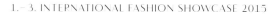

3.

1.–3. INTERNATIONAL FASHION SHOWCASE 2015

JAMES DAWE | COLLAGE

4.

5.

6.

4. & 5. PUPE LONDON, ELECTPIC BEACH HEPO 6. INTEPNATIONAL FASHION SHOWCASE 2015

2.

3.

ELISE
HURST
—

1. IMAGINE THE STORIES 2. THE WAITING SKY 3. THE CROW DOCTOR

1.

STORYTELLING

MERIJN
HOS
—

1. SUMMER COVER OF FINANCIEEL DAGBLAD 2. DE MORGEN

JON
KLASSEN
—

1. VISA FALLS 2. THIS IS NOT MY HAT 3. ICE AGE

HIFU
MIYO
—

1.

2.

3.

4.

1. – 4. FRANCE 365 5. DAS MAGAZIN

2.

3.

4.

1. DAS MAGAZIN 2.–4. FRANCE 365

TINY BOP'S
ROBOT FACTORY
—

1.

2.

1. – 4. PLANTS

STOPYTELLING

3.

4.

1.

2.

1. – 3. PLANTS

1.

OWEN
DAVEY
—

1. & 2. MAD ABOUT MONKEYS – NOBROW PRESS

STORYTELLING

2.

BJØRN
RUNE LIE
—

3.

2.

4.

1. HIUT DENIM TEEPEE 2. SHAKLETON'S 3. DEUS BIKER 4. JACKSON + PYE RESTAURANT MENU

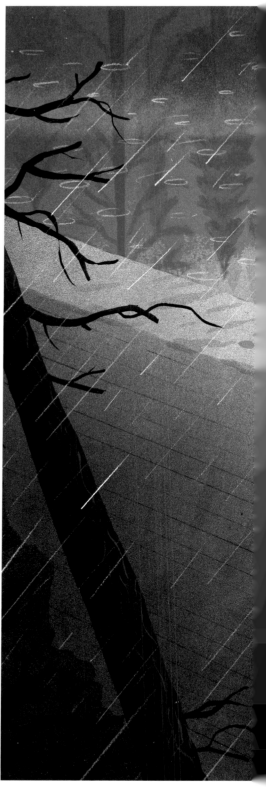

1. VOLVO 2. CLASSROOM 3. ON THE DAM

BJØRN RUNE LIE | STORYTELLING

OWEN
GATLEY
—

1. SKI SEASON ACTIVITIES 2. SKIING IN THE ALPS

STOPYTELLING

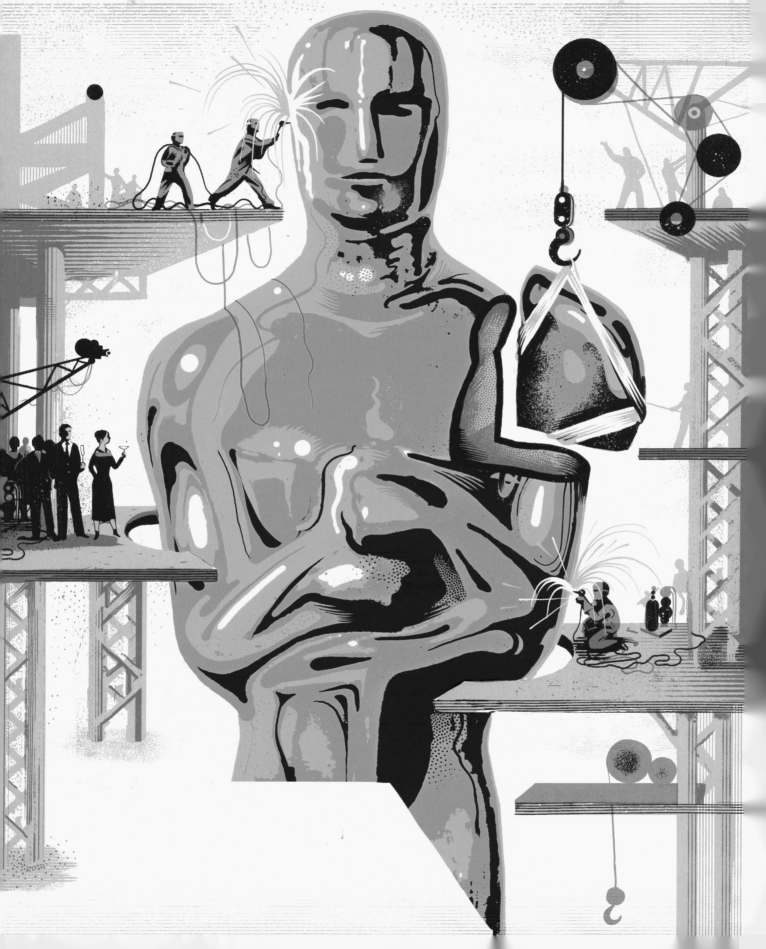

ICINORI

—

1. OSCAR 2. FACTORY

1. IN THE SHELL 2. FACTORY 3. & 4. ELLE TOURNE COMME ÇA 5. PÉCHÉS CHAPITEAUX 6. THE PACE

1. CANOE 2. JACCO

1.

jacco
gardner

LUNDI 8 AVRIL 2013
20H • TROC'AFÉ
8 FAUBOURG DE SAVERNE STRASBOURG
8€ LOC • 9€ SOIR • CONCERT PANIMIX

PANIMIX
DJ·SET

2.

BARBARA
DZIADOSZ
—

1.

2.

3.

4.

1. WOODPECKER 2. COLD 3. JUNGLE 4. DINOSAURS 5. ICE

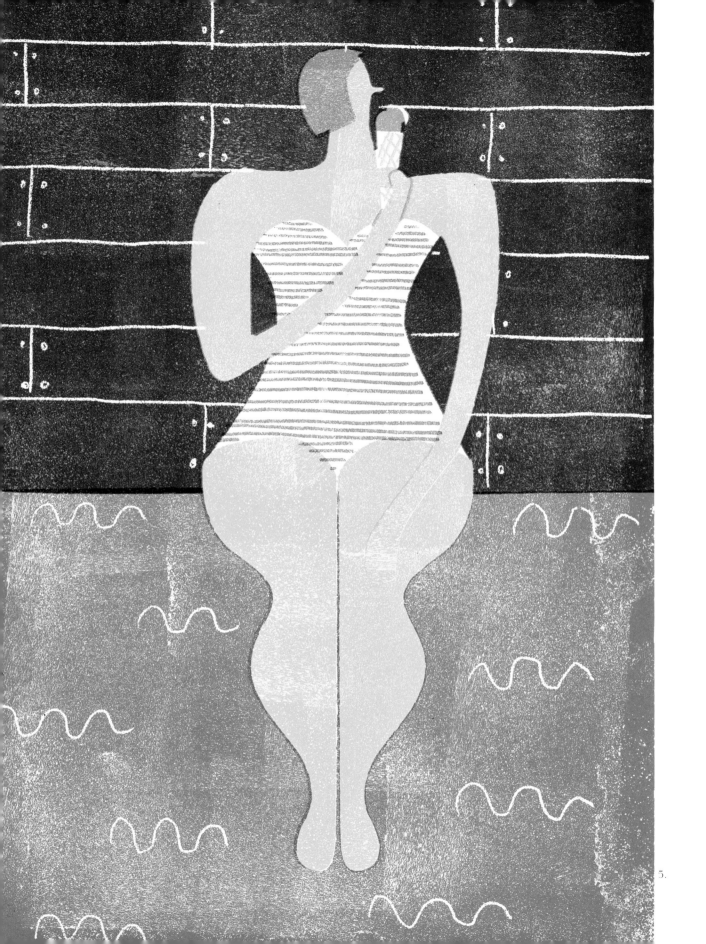

5.

BARBARA DZIADOSZ | STOPYTELLING

2 red onion

porcini mushrooms

1 tin cannellini beans

2 tablespoons brown sugar

2 tablespoons smoked paprika

2 fresh chilis

30g fresh coriander

AMERICAN

2 yellow peppers

1 tablespoon fennel seeds

1 tablespoon coriander seeds

2 tins tomatoes

1 tin corn

150ml balsamic vinegar

1 butternut squash

salt   pepper

2 red peppers

Chili

2.

reaux

CONSERVERIE

3.

PATISSERIE

4.

Pizza

thyme   rosemary

Oro Di Parma

garlic

tomato puree   parmesan   tinned tomatoes

pepper   salt

mozzarella   rucola   oregano

basil

5.

1. PAELLA 2. CHILI 3. MACKEPELS 4. PATISSEPIE 5. PIZZA

CHRIS
HAUGHTON
—

3.

2.

1. A BIT LOST 2. HATMONKEY 3. A BIT LOST 4. SHH

4.

2.

3.

1. HATMONKEY 2. A BIT LOST 3. SHH

JÖNS
MELLGREN
—

1. – 3. ELSA AND THE NIGHT

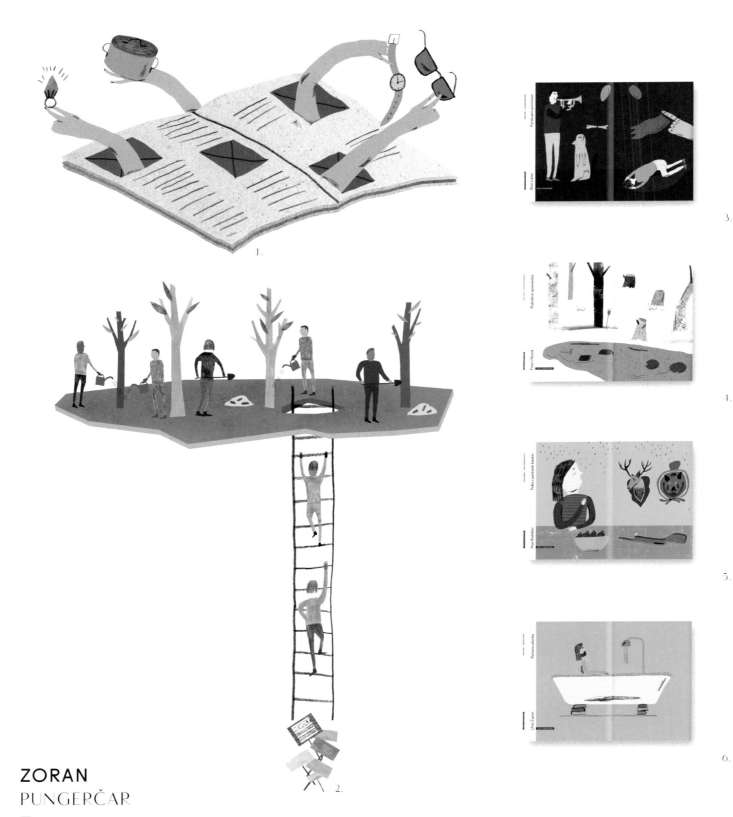

ZORAN
PUNGERČAR
—

1. & 2. EDITORIAL ILLUSTRATIONS FOR NEWSPAPER DELO 3. PRIČAKUJEM POZORNOST 4. PODNEBNE SPREMEMBE
5. POLKA S PEŠČENIH BANKIN 6. POČASNA PLOVBA 7. NORA GREGOR

INDEX

MICHAEL
MORGENSTERN
—

MIGUEL ANGEL
VALDIVIA
—

MIKE
LOWERY
—

MIREILLE
FAUCHON
—

MISTER
MOURAO
—

N
NAJA
CONRAD-HANSEN
—

O
OLIMPIA
ZAGNOLI
—

ORIANA
FENWICK
—

OWEN
DAVEY
—

OWEN
GATLEY
—

P
PARTERRE
DE ROIS
—

PATRICK
MORGAN
—

PAUL
REILLY
—

PAULA
SANZ CABALLERO
—

PETER
GRUNDY
—

PETER
HORVATH
—

THOMAS
DANTHONY
—

TIM
LAING
—

TINA
BERNING
—

TINY BOP'S
ROBOT FACTORY
—

TOM
HAUGOMAT
—

TONI
HALONEN
—

Z

ZORAN
PUNGERČAR
—

illusive

CONTEMPORARY
ILLUSTRATION
PART FOUR

This book was conceived, edited, and designed by Gestalten.
Edited by Robert Klanten and John O'Reilly
Texts written by John O'Reilly
Texts edited by Noelia Hobeika
Proofreading by
Transparent Language Solutions and Rachel Sampson

Layout and design by Michelle Kliem
Front cover picture by Andreas Lie
Back cover photography (top to bottom):
Hifu Miyo, Liselotte Watkins, Peter Horvath, Hattie Newman,
Toni Halonen, Kindred Studio, Cristina Amodeo
Typeface: Ogaki CE by Áron Jancsó, Vanitas by Michael Jarboe,
Fugue by Radim Peško

Printed by Offsetdruckerei Karl Grammlich GmbH, Pliezhausen
Made in Germany
Published by Gestalten, Berlin 2015
ISBN 978-3-89955-587-5

For more information, please visit
gestalten.com.

Bibliographic information published by the Deutsche Nationalbibliothek:
The Deutsche Nationalbibliothek lists this publication in the Deutsche Nationalbibliografie;
detailed bibliographic data are available online at http://dnb.d-nb.de.

None of the content in this book was published in exchange for payment by commercial
parties or designers; Gestalten selected all included work based solely on its artistic merit.

This book was printed on paper certified according to the standard of FSC®.